AND THEY CAME TO PASS

AND THEY CAME TO PASS

BYU'S AMAZING STRING OF ALL-AMERICAN QB'S

LEE BENSON

Deseret Book Company
Salt Lake City, Utah

For my dad

No part of this book may be reproduced in any
form or by any means without permission in writing
from the publisher, Deseret Book Company,
P.O. Box 30178, Salt Lake City, Utah 84130.
Deseret Book is a registered trademark of
Deseret Book Company.

First printing August 1988

Library of Congress Cataloging-in-Publication Data

Benson, Lee, 1948–
    And they came to pass / Lee Benson.
      p. cm.
    Includes index.
    ISBN 0-87579-155-7 : $10.95 (est.)
      1. Football players—United States—Biography. 2. Quarterback
(Football) 3. Brigham Young University—Football. I. Title.
GV939.A1B39   1988
796.332'092'2—dc19
[B]   88-15504
                                          CIP

Contents

Acknowledgments

This book would not have been possible without the help of many people. There were the quarterbacks themselves, who generously told me how it was. There were the parents — Bill and Lois Sheide, Stan and Lois Nielsen, Doug and Carroll Wilson, Jim and Roberta McMahon, LeGrande and Sherry Young, and Lou and Elva Bosco — who spoke long into the night on their favorite subjects. There were Greg Sheide, Mike McMahon, Mike Young and John Bosco, brothers who told it straight. There were the coaches — Dewey Warren, Doug Scovil, Ted Tollner, Mike Holmgren and LaVell Edwards especially — who made it complete. And there was Ralph Zobell, who was the real historian.

Three things can happen when you pass — and one of them is good.

Prologue

This wasn't the way Gifford Nielsen imagined it would be.

Growing up two blocks from the campus of Brigham Young University, he often thought of one day playing for the Cougars. It helped him make it through algebra at Provo's Farrer Junior High School, daydreaming of last-second baskets hitting nothing but net. He liked basketball more than he liked algebra. He liked basketball more than he liked *anything*. At Provo High School he had been on a basketball team that won thirty-four straight games, and he had been named the most valuable high school basketball player in the state of Utah.

So when the college across the street had given him a scholarship to play basketball, he'd just known it couldn't get any better than this.

He was right. It hadn't gotten any better. Major college basketball was a struggle. He'd started on the BYU varsity as a freshman and as a sophomore had averaged 8.5 points a game; but the teams lost more games than they won. And at 6'5" he was an awkward height — too big for guard, too small for forward. He guessed he wasn't destined for basketball greatness.

So now here he was, playing football. More or less. In the fall of 1975 he was BYU's third-string quarterback.

Midway through the fourth game of the season, at home against New Mexico, his uniform was so clean it was embarrassing. The block numeral 14, in white, stood out in sharp contrast against the blue jersey. He felt tempted to reach down and smear some dirt across the front.

More embarrassing, he was third-string on a bad team. The Cougars were already 0-3 and heading fast for 0 and 4. New Mexico was ahead 12-0 late in the third quarter. People who had driven to the night game from Salt Lake City were already heading toward the exits to get a jump on the trip home. The audience of 25,140 was thinning fast.

On the sidelines, BYU head coach LaVell Edwards wouldn't have minded leaving, either. His coaching career was twenty-six games old; and with no thanks to this season's winless start, he was batting below .500 with a 12-13-1 lifetime mark. The radical passing system he'd established, and had early success with during quarterback Gary Sheide's two seasons, was looking like another football gimmick gone bad.

But he couldn't leave, so he looked down the bench and, on an impulse, waved Nielsen into the game. The starting quarterback, Mark Giles, was injured, and his backup, Jeff Duva, was having little success.

Nielsen pointed at himself.

"Me?" he asked.

Edwards nodded.

Gifford Nielsen — a basketball player gone AWOL — trotted to the middle of Cougar Stadium. No one, except for Gifford's father, Stan, said, "Here comes Giff." And he only whispered it, like a warning.

It happened so fast that it took a lot of people by surprise — including the New Mexico defense. One minute and nine seconds later, BYU completed a four-play, sixty-seven-yard drive with a Nielsen-to-Dave Lowry touchdown pass. New Mexico 12, BYU 7. Six minutes later, after New Mexico countered with a field goal, BYU capped an eighty-yard drive with a Nielsen-to-Jeff Blanc touchdown pass. New Mexico 15, BYU 13.

Then came the clincher. Nielsen completed three passes in four attempts to set up Dave Taylor's thirty-yard winning field goal with 1:46 left in the game. Final score: BYU 16, New Mexico 15. In just over sixteen minutes, Gifford Nielsen had thrown twelve passes and completed ten of them — and BYU had found a way to win.

LaVell Edwards' coaching record would never come remotely close to the .500-level again, and BYU football would never be the same again.

It had come to pass.

BYU would continue on a passing tear unparalleled in the history of collegiate football. From 1973 through 1985 the Cougars would win 122 games while losing only thirty-six, and would climax their climb into the nation's football consciousness by winning the national championship in 1984. What quarterbacks Gary Sheide and Gifford Nielsen got started, Marc Wilson, Jim McMahon, Steve Young, and Robbie Bosco kept going, and going, and going. This is their story.

IN THE BEGINNING

*D*on *Rydalch looked in his* rearview mirror as Rexburg, Idaho, faded into the distance. He sighed nostalgically. This was not an easy move. He had been born near Rexburg, in Newdale, the grain capital of the world, and when he became a football coach he'd gone to work at Ricks Junior College in Rexburg. For five of the past six years he had been the Vikings' head coach. His wide-open teams — they passed as much as a third of the time — had an overall record of 24-20, an accomplishment that attracted the attention of the new head coach at Brigham Young University in Provo, Utah.

It was the spring of 1972 and BYU had hired LaVell Edwards to replace Tommy Hudspeth. Edwards' choice as his quarterback coach, and the man who would set up his offense, was Ricks College's Don Rydalch.

Rydalch was flattered by the offer. A position on the staff at a four-year school was the natural next step up the coaching ladder. But he was also ambivalent about leaving. Rexburg was his home. He liked the fishing and the hunting and his status in the community; and his wife and ten children weren't at all anxious to leave. There was also the possibility that the Edwards era wouldn't

1

last long at BYU, where they changed coaches at roughly the same rate Elizabeth Taylor changed husbands. He agonized over his decision.

Finally he called Edwards and said he'd be in Provo in the morning.

Rydalch loaded his Ford sedan and drove out of town, past the bowling alley and Bill's Cafe and the Sinclair station. As he approached the Snake River and the Lorenzo Bridge south of town, he bid a silent adieu and pushed down on the gas—and never made it to the other side.

The bridge had iced over from a snowstorm the night before, and a car coming from the south veered out of control, crossed the center line, and slammed head-on into Rydalch's Ford.

He woke up in the Madison Memorial Hospital, his knee and head cut badly. He wasn't going anywhere for a few days—which gave him time to reassess the direction of his life.

Rydalch had known it would be hard leaving Rexburg. He hadn't realized it would be *that* hard.

He called Edwards, who was starting spring practice in Provo, and said he was sorry but he'd have to turn down the job.

Rydalch had been Edwards' Plan A. He didn't have a Plan B. The Cougars went through the spring without a quarterback coach.

After spring practice, Jim Criner, the BYU assistant coach in charge of linebackers, went to a football clinic in Tennessee to study the Volunteers' new bubble defense. There he became acquainted with a twenty-seven-year-old University of Tennessee assistant coach named Dewey Warren, also known, from his All-American days as a quarterback at Tennessee and during a brief professional career with the Cincinnati Bengals and Las Vegas Cowboys, as "The Swamp Rat."

Warren, a native of Savannah, Georgia, was Tennessee's assistant freshman coach, and he liked nothing better than throwing the football. "If you've got a running play, you can make a passing play out of it," was The Swamp Rat's philosophy. He had played for Bill Walsh, the notorious, pass-minded quarterback coach when he'd been at Cincinnati. The Swamp Rat was flamboyant and cocky

2

and sure of himself, and he impressed Criner, who got on the phone and called the office.

"LaVell," he said, "I think you ought to talk to this guy."

Edwards flew Warren to Provo over the July 4th weekend. Pat Boone was performing in the BYU stadium and fireworks were going off when Edwards tossed Warren a large notebook filled with blank pages.

"Write us up an offense," he said. "And by the way, you're hired."

The Swamp Rat was sitting on a coaches' dream. He was in only his third year as a coach, and he had full authority to set up a major college offense.

During the month before the players reported for August workouts, he invented an offense that was the image of himself, and one the likes of which no one had ever seen.

"We'll throw to the backs, and hit seams, and go after the deep curl areas," he explained to his new boss. "And we'll take what they give us. We won't try to hit the home run every time." It all sounded fine to Edwards, a coach with a defensive background. It also sounded fine to the players, who, when they arrived, took a great interest in their new offense. Everyone was involved — the backs, the receivers, the quarterback, the line, everyone. Warren was suggesting that they establish a passing game first, and run off of it occasionally — if they felt like it.

Other than being the direct opposite of traditional football thinking, there was nothing unusual about his approach.

So the Cougars went to the air. Although not immediately. That first season they had a running back named "Fleet" Pete Van Valkenburg. He wasn't really all that fleet, but he had a knack for never falling down until it was absolutely necessary. He led the nation in rushing in 1972, taking a school-record 232 handoffs from quarterbacks Bill August and Dave Terry, two players who weren't exactly what Warren's state-of-the-art passing offense had in mind. "They were good athletes, just not great throwers," said Warren. "But the next year we lost Van Valkenburg and picked up this junior college kid, Gary Sheide. He was the spitting image of Joe Namath. He looked like him, talked like him, hunched over like him."

And ended up playing a lot like him.

3

GARY SHEIDE

"ROCK THE BOAT BABY"
— *The Hues Corporation, 1973*

*I*t *was just minutes* before the start of the 1974 Fiesta Bowl. Gary Sheide walked over and put his arm around the shoulder of his brother Greg, who was standing on the sidelines in Sun Devil Stadium, even if he wasn't supposed to be.

"We're going to score fifty points today," said Gary, checking back a smile. "I can't believe these guys. They don't know how to stop us."

"They" were the football players from Oklahoma State University, the team the Fiesta Bowl had chosen to play against Brigham Young University, the champion of the Western Athletic Conference (WAC).

Because this was BYU's first bowl appearance ever, a lot of experts had picked the OSU Cowboys to win. But all week long Sheide, the BYU quarterback, had studied films of the Cowboys. He was convinced that — after spending the season playing in the run-oriented Big 8 Conference — they had not seen anything like what BYU would throw at them. He'd said nothing publicly, preferring to play his hand, as he said, "like

4

a country hayseed." But he privately told some team-mates as well as his brother Greg, with whom he shared everything, that he thought Oklahoma State wouldn't have either a clue or a chance.

After completing four of his first five passes for forty-three yards in the first ten minutes of play — passes that had already set up two BYU field goals for a quick 6-0 lead — he was convinced. And feeling no pain.

As futures go, they couldn't look much brighter than this.

To end the 1974 regular season, Sheide had rallied BYU to seven straight wins after an 0-3-1 start. His completion percentage of 60.3 was the fourth best in NCAA history. In twenty games he had set a con-ference record with 358 completions, breaking a record it had taken Danny White of Arizona State thirty-two games to set.

He was already ticketed for the Hula Bowl in Ha-waii, an all-star game for seniors, where he had been named the starter for the West team. It seemed every-body wanted Sheide. Just two weeks earlier, an agent named Irwin Weiner had flown him to New York City. Actually he'd flown both Gary and Greg back. "My brother's going to be my business agent," Gary had told Weiner. "If I'm coming, so is he."

"What's he going to do, wipe your nose?" sneered Weiner, who sent the two airline tickets to Provo just the same.

In New York the brothers were picked up by a stretch limo and taken to the Biltmore Hotel, where Weiner had arranged for a suite. "Order anything you like from room service," he told them. The first thing Gary did was phone down for a bowl of cashews. They were twelve dollars. He signed for them and added a five-dollar tip.

"He said anything we wanted," Gary said to Greg.

As agents go, Weiner was in the big leagues. He

had Julius Erving and Walt Frazier and George McGinnis at the time, and took calls from Erving and Frazier — or so he said — while the Sheide brothers were in his office the next morning.

Weiner leaned across his desk, his gold chain falling forward, looked Gary Sheide in the eye, and told him he was projected to be selected third in the upcoming NFL draft. And with his help they could look realistically at a six-figure signing bonus.

The Sheides tried not to gulp perceptively. At the time they were paying forty-nine dollars a month for the apartment they shared in Provo.

Life had always been good, but this was getting ridiculous.

ANTIOCH, CALIFORNIA
1952-1972

Antioch, California, where Gary Sheide grew up, is a community of thirty thousand located thirty miles from San Francisco, fifty miles from Sacramento, and right next to the Sacramento River on the San Joaquin Delta, where Gary spent a good deal of his time. Baseball was his first love, and football was where he would make his mark; but his favorite place was on the banks of the Sacramento, digging clams and fishing for catfish and, occasionally, striped bass and steelhead. When he eventually wound up going to college in Provo, Utah, of all places, it was the trout in the Provo River and Strawberry Reservoir that clinched the deal.

Not that it was easy to fish the Sacramento, at least not in the best spots. The prime fishing holes were located on private land owned by the two companies that made Antioch economically possible — Crown Zellerbach and Kaiser. To get to the Crown Zellerbach property, Gary and Greg had to make their way past three fences and a guard dog, which tended to make it all the more worthwhile.

Greg was born first. He was eleven months older and would always be taller, topping out at 6'5" to Gary's 6'2". But Gary was bigger, almost from the start, and the brothers became as close as twins. They had a paper route together. They shared the same room. Marty, a third brother, came along six years later, and that was his problem. When he was old enough to play football he was the designated center. One time he broke his leg, another time he broke his hand.

Bill Sheide drove an ice cream truck for Berkeley Farms and rarely could make it from the truck to the house when he came home at the end of the day. He'd either have a baseball or a football or a basketball or a fishing pole flung at him, and he could do everything but say no. Bill had played semi-pro basketball in the thirties for Stroms Clothiers in Oakland, his hometown, and he had an affection for sports. When he married Lois Milkert in 1950 in Reno they first settled in Concord, eleven miles to the southwest; but there were no Little League programs there so they moved to Antioch, to the house on Marie Street, a mile from the river.

The living in Antioch was easy. Stressless. Laid-back. The brothers played all the sports, but practice was often interrupted for fishing or other distractions, and sometimes, in the summer, by an eight-hour shift at the paper mill.

Gary played sports on instinct. He was never high on organized practice or particularly anxious to take orders. He was instinctive with other things, too, such as music. He taught himself the saxophone, and the guitar, and the piano. One night, after hearing the organ player at an Oakland A's baseball game, he came home and bought an electric organ, set it up in the front room, and practiced steadily for a week. By the time he was finished he could play any popular song he wanted. He asked for requests.

Schoolwork also came naturally. His high school grades at Antioch High School were good enough to get him into the Ivy League schools and/or Stanford, where he was offered a scholarship. At BYU, in between football practice and fishing, he would carry a 3.23 grade point average and make the all-conference academic team.

Still, he had a kind of nonchalance about him. "His attitude was that if it works out, fine, if it doesn't, there's always fishing," is how Bill Sheide explained it.

But in the heat of competition he could be adamant about winning. Being an underdog never mattered, and neither did past history. When he was a junior and the quarterback at Antioch High, the Panthers traveled to Pittsburg High for a game against a traditional area powerhouse they hadn't beaten in football in twenty-two years. Gary played his best game of the season and Antioch won 20-0. Later that school year, during basketball season, Sheide scored a tip-in with one second remaining in the third overtime as Antioch beat Pittsburg for the first time in twelve years.

This did not make Gary Sheide the Man of the Year in Pittsburg; and by his senior season, when it was time again for the annual Antioch-Pittsburg football game, this time in Antioch, he was square in the center of the rivalry.

On the Wednesday before the game he was playing the organ in the front room when the phone rang.

"Take the field Friday and you're dead," said the voice on the other end.

"Who was that?" asked Gary's mother from the kitchen.

"Uh, nobody."

The phone rang again. It was the same caller, with the same message.

The calls kept up until the day of the game, when fans from Pittsburg began arriving in Antioch at 3:00 P.M. — for an 8:00 P.M. kickoff. Football was not something they took lightly in Pittsburg.

On Antioch's first possession, Gary marched the Panthers the length of the field for a touchdown. He next raised both arms in the air and paraded that way in front of the Pittsburg fans. No other shots were fired. Antioch went on to a 45-38 win.

Gary had a problem backing down. When he was a sophomore at Antioch High, he was promoted to the varsity basketball team — a first in the school's history — and became a starter on a senior-oriented squad that included his brother Greg. During a midseason game with Pleasant Hill, a school that featured Vince Udjur, a

6'5" center who was maybe the best player in the area and definitely the most physical, Gary took a sharp elbow from Udjur. He turned away limping. Antioch coach Mario Tonin called time out.

"What's wrong?" the coach asked.

"He elbowed me," said Gary. "He elbowed me hard."

He got his breath.

"Let me just hit him, one time."

His older teammates did a double take. Did he know who that was? That was Vince Udjur, the league enforcer, and Gary Sheide was a *sophomore*.

"Don't hit him," said the coach.

As the game resumed with a jump ball, Gary did something unconventional. Instead of jumping for the ball he jumped for Udjur, slamming him to the floor. Udjur got up and took a swing. Sheide took two and chased Udjur to the middle of the court, where the police grabbed Gary from behind. He turned to the police and in his most polite voice said, "I'm calmed down now, I'm all right." When they let him go he chased Udjur out of the gym.

After that, a lot of people thought football was the perfect sport for Gary Sheide. But even though he played quarterback, with success, as both a sophomore and a junior, by his senior year of high school he almost quit. He had his reasons. He hated practice, for one thing. For another, they were switching the Antioch offense to the new rage of the day, the wishbone, which meant he would pass less frequently. He was a high school holdout until just before practice began in the fall of 1970, when peer pressure won him over and he came back to play football for what he thought would be the last time.

If he was going to play a sport in college, and he hoped as a professional, it was baseball. The Baltimore Orioles drafted him out of high school, as a shortstop, in the late rounds. Sheide had range, he had good speed, he had a strong arm, and he could hit with power. He and another shortstop—Kiko Garcia—were considered the area's top pro prospects.

Garcia did go on to play for the Orioles. Sheide went another direction.

9

While his right arm was his number-one asset, it was also his number-one nemesis. Keeping it healthy was a full-time job. He hyperextended his right shoulder while playing basketball when he was an eighth-grader, and it triggered a chain of injuries through high school and into college, finally culminating with a costly one his first year at Diablo Valley Junior College—where Sheide had enrolled upon the advice of his high school baseball coach, Babe Atkinson, who also worked as a scout for the Orioles.

At Diablo Valley, Sheide could improve his baseball skills, get a start on his education while playing for a good college program, and probably improve his order in the draft. But by choosing a junior college, Sheide turned down hundreds of major college scholarship offers in all three sports. In football he had at least one offer from every major conference in the country, including BYU. LaVell Edwards, then an assistant coach to Tommy Hudspeth, had personally recruited Sheide in 1970.

As a freshman in the fall of 1971 at Diablo Valley, after a summer of baseball, Sheide was content to never play competitive football again. But, by coincidence, Diablo Valley's two top quarterbacks were injured during August workouts. Several players on the team had been Sheide's teammates at Antioch, and they urged him to come out and play. He declined. They sent the coach over. Sheide still declined. Then the entire coaching staff went over.

By this time two-a-days were nearly finished, which made him more receptive. He told coach Sam DeVito he'd play on condition.

"What condition?" asked DeVito.

These were Sheide's terms: first, he wouldn't have to play bull-in-the-ring, a barbaric sort of drill where one player is surrounded by linemen and has to make his way out of the circle; second, he wouldn't have contact in practice (he had a baseball career to think about); third, he could spend practice working with his receivers; and fourth, he could pass all he wanted.

The coach agreed.

Three games later, all lopsided wins, Diablo Valley was ranked number two among the country's junior colleges.

But in the fourth game Sheide met his nemesis. A defensive lineman fell on his right wrist and the navicular bone broke. Not having an intact navicular bone—the bone that connects the thumb to the hand—is like not having a trigger in a gun. The same injury had cost the New York Jets' Joe Namath a full season in the pros. Sheide knew that because Namath was his idol. That was the only consolation.

His right hand was in a cast for six months. He couldn't play baseball the next spring, which meant he wasn't drafted, and he could see that career quickly dying. So for the first time Sheide thought seriously about football. He reasoned that if he could have a good sophomore season at Diablo Valley, he could get a scholarship at a major university and pay for his schooling.

He went through two-a-days that next August and, when the season began, picked up where he'd left off. Diablo Valley broke to another 3-0 start, just like the year before; but also, just like the year before, Sheide broke his right hand. This time it was the radius bone. He was in a cast for eight weeks, the duration of the season.

Sheide was undefeated after two years in junior college football, but he'd played only six games. Recruiters looked at him like he was a crap table. They backed off. They hedged. He visited the University of Washington, a good fishing area, where they said they wanted him to redshirt because they had a veteran quarterback, Sonny Sixkiller, who would be the starter.

"What if I'm better?" asked Sheide, who did not want to redshirt and turned down the Huskies' offer.

He visited the Naval Academy and was impressed. But he was more impressed by all the attention he was receiving, still, from Brigham Young University, a school he knew nothing about. Certainly the BYU Cougars were not, at the time, the subject of a schoolboy quarterback's daydreams.

"I knew it was a church school," said Sheide. "But I didn't know what church."

He paid a recruiting visit to Provo for the BYU-Wyoming game in 1972, LaVell Edwards' first year as head coach and Dewey Warren's first year as quarterback coach. He went fishing on the Provo River. He talked to Edwards. He talked to Warren, whose table manners went something along the lines of "pass the football please." He was skeptical about just how committed the Cougars were to the passing game they kept talking about. Their running back, Pete Van Valkenburg, was leading the nation in rushing. But Warren explained that it was a revolutionary system they were developing, and they were looking for the right kind of quarterback to drive the car.

Sheide had a feeling.

He said they should expect him in the spring.

1973

He came to Provo for the spring semester of 1973 in a yellow 1967 Ford Fairline packed to the roof. After moving into the dormitory at Deseret Towers, Gary Sheide soon discovered just how much of a church school he'd signed on with. The first Sunday there he got up and walked to the dorm cafeteria for breakfast. The doors were locked. It was fast Sunday for the Mormons.

Other realities of life surfaced. He reported to spring workouts and found that not only was he desperately wanted by the Cougars — as they'd said in their recruiting pitch — but so were seven other quarterbacks. Obviously, Edwards and Warren were taking no chances. Practice was like a sunny day at the beach. Everybody was there. The eight quarterbacks would stand in a line and wait their turn to run the offense. Gary called Greg in California. He said the jury was still out on this place, but the fishing was good.

By the fall semester Greg had transferred to BYU. The brothers had shared a room too long to be separated now. Along with two other Californians — Tim Mahoney, a fullback on the football team, and John Ryan — they rented an apartment at the University Villa apartments not far from campus. For silverware they "borrowed" utensils from JB's on University Avenue, the restaurant where they'd eaten their first meal.

BYU had more rules and regulations than they were accustomed to. But they could be circumvented. At registration the Sheides happened to see a stack of "A" parking stickers in the registrar's office. They weren't greedy. They took four. For the first month of school, until security got onto them, they parked in spaces reserved for faculty, deans, General Authorities, and the university president.

To get around what they thought were rather un-California hair policies — this was the age of Haight-Ashbury and John Lennon — they wet their hair down and slicked it behind their ears before registering for classes, and then went home and blew it dry.

Never an early riser, Gary set himself up on the "2:00 to 2:00" schedule. He never scheduled a class before two o'clock in the afternoon. After football practice, when there was enough light, he went fishing.

He acquired a taste for Hi-Spot hamburgers — mainly because they were five for a dollar. He, Greg, Mahoney and Ryan flipped nightly to see who would make the Hi-Spot run for twenty burgers. His best friend became Jay Miller, another Californian and a wide receiver who would catch one hundred passes the first year he teamed up with Sheide. When they roomed together Miller had a habit of writing girls' names and telephone numbers on the wall by the phone. Sheide would call a number, any number.

"He'd say, 'Hi, this is Jay,' and then he'd say things to make them think I was an idiot," remembers Miller.

In his off-the-wall way, Gary Sheide adapted quickly to his new environment. He made himself right at home. "I had never seen so many friendly people," he said, "or so many beautiful girls."

By the end of his senior year he had married one of them, his wife Sherree, and joined the Mormon church.

Such was the state of BYU football when Gary Sheide discovered Hi-Spot hamburgers in the year nineteen hundred and seventy-three:

• The program had existed since 1922, not counting the war years when the sport was discontinued. (Actually, football began at BYU around the turn of the century, but a player was killed and that ended that.)

• In forty-eight official seasons the Cougars had won 180 games and lost 239. Since the end of the war they had won 104 games and lost 163.

• They had managed sixteen seasons with records above .500, or one every three years. Ironically, their only time of relative prosperity had come when all else was miserable, during the Depression. Seven of their winning seasons occurred between 1929 and 1939.

• They had gone through eleven coaches, or roughly one every four and a half years. Most had not left of their own free will.

• Among their traditions was an annual loss to the University of Utah. In forty-eight years against the Utes—an arch-rival in name only—they were 6-39-3.

• In forty-eight years against their other instate rival, Utah State, they were 16-29-3. Their grand total instate record was 22-68-6.

• They had won one conference championship in forty-eight years (the WAC title in 1966).

• They had never been nationally ranked.

• They had never beaten a team that was nationally ranked, or a team that was even close to being ranked.

• They had never been invited to a bowl game.

• And they had an inferiority complex thicker than the smog coming out of the smokestacks at nearby Geneva Steel.

No one knew exactly why the Cougars were so inept at football. There were many theories, chief among them that a school of Mormon boys who were taught to love their neighbor and never hurt, maim, injure or cripple a fellow human being could not expect to fare well in a contact sport. How could you sack the quarterback and turn the other cheek at the same time? BYU's success in basketball, a noncontact sport, tended to validate this theory. As bad as the football teams were, the basketball teams were good. They had won the National Invitation Tournament twice—when the NIT meant something—and they were the resident bully of the WAC. In the first ten years of the conference's existence, BYU had already won five basketball championships.

In 1972 a twenty-three-thousand-seat arena, the Marriott Activities Center, had been opened on campus. Even with that many seats, tickets to basketball games were as scarce as football tickets were plentiful.

To counteract the Mormon theory in football, steps were occasionally taken. A non-Mormon coach named Hal Kopp was hired out of the East in 1956. But he didn't get along well with the administration and, despite showing promise with a 13-14-3 record, was fired after three seasons. Then the Cougars got desperate and hired the enemy, an ex-University of Utah star named Tally Stevens, who had coached East High School in Salt Lake City to the Utah state championship. Stevens endured two three-win seasons before he was released.

In 1964 BYU hired Tommy Hudspeth, an Oklahoman who brought the Marines with him. Literally. Hudspeth recruited several Marine veterans, including wide receiver Phil Odle, who became an All-American in 1967. Hudspeth's Marines brought a new look, not to mention the school's first conference championship, to BYU in 1966 when they went 8-2 and ran the flag up against the University of Utah, 35-13. But by 1971, after two straight losing seasons, Hudspeth—a man prone to throwing postgame temper tantrums, some of them publicly on his postgame radio show—had worn out his welcome. It was one thing to lose. It was another to cry about it.

When it came time to make a coaching change in 1972, Woody Hayes and Bear Bryant didn't apply and the Cougars were out of ideas, so they stayed in-house. They hired Hudspeth's defensive coordinator, R. LaVell Edwards, forty-one, who had been at the school since 1962 and had been on the staffs of both Hal Mitchell and Hudspeth. In his ten seasons as an assistant coach Edwards had seen the Cougars win forty-five games and lose fifty-six. Prior to that he had been the head coach at Granite High School in Salt Lake City for eight years, where his teams went 18-25-1 in league play and had only two winning seasons.

When Edwards got the job at BYU neither he nor his new employer were kidding themselves. He was not Amos Alonzo

Stagg. In eighteen seasons as a coach he'd been associated with just six winning seasons.

"I know only one thing," he told his staff, "we've got to do something different."

As an assistant coach Edwards had been inspired by BYU's season in 1966, the Cougars' best ever, when they broke through the abyss long enough to go 8-2, beat Utah, and win the WAC. That year they had Virgil ("The Blue Darter") Carter at quarterback. Carter was a passer first and a passer second, and Hudspeth had turned him loose, unwittingly. Without much of an organized offensive scheme, BYU had still beaten teams and done things never done before. The beginning of an offensive theory had formed in Edwards' mind. The only way a forlorn program such as BYU's could compete was to throw the football, and to recruit people who knew how to throw it. As an assistant coach sitting in Gary Sheide's home in Antioch, California, in 1970 — before either of them knew what was to come — he had said as much. That was why the Cougars needed Bill and Lois Sheide's boy. He knew how to pass the football.

Edwards had the vision. When Dewey Warren arrived from Tennessee, he added the focus. They would be the New Cougars. They would drop back. They would control the underneath coverage by throwing to the backs when needed and handcuffing the linebackers. They would flood receivers all over the field, exploiting seams in the defense while attacking the standard zone defenses of the day. They would have a checkoff system for the quarterback — if the primary receiver was covered he would look immediately to his first option, then his second option, and so on. And they would develop a pass-blocking scheme on the offensive line to give it enough time to work.

Instead of going after the players everyone else was after — the recruits BYU rarely got, the running backs with 4.4 speed and the 6'4" linebackers — they would recruit players who could throw and catch, and a few large (not necessarily quick) linemen who could stand in front of the quarterback and make like a moat.

It would all sound simple fifteen years later. But in 1972 nobody was doing it. Anywhere. Not when Darrell Royal, the eminent

16

coach at Texas, was saying, "Three things can happen when you pass, and two of them are bad," and he was being quoted on the "Tonight Show."

Throughout the history of football the forward pass had been primarily a gimmick. It first came to prominence in 1913 when a little-known Catholic school in Indiana called Notre Dame used it to beat Army. The Notre Dame quarterback, Gus Dorais, spent all summer on the shores of Lake Erie, where he was working at a summer resort, throwing passes to his end, Knute Rockne. When the Irish traveled to West Point and unveiled their passing attack it was akin to the Trojans coming out of the horse. Army was taken completely by surprise and lost, 35-13.

But as Notre Dame rounded into a national powerhouse, and attracted the fast, swift recruits to its campus in South Bend, the Irish eschewed the forward pass and went back to a traditional running attack. The pass was put back on the shelf to be fooled around with only occasionally by down-and-outers looking for a quick fix. Not until another church school and football lightweight came along in 1973 was the pass again looked at seriously for salvation.

Similar to computers and microwave ovens, what BYU introduced in the early 1970s was something no one had seen before.

Even the inventors didn't know if it would work. Edwards and Warren were scientists in a test lab. To have any kind of a chance they knew they needed the right quarterback. In 1972, their first year together, they didn't think they had one. And because they had no burning desire to be the laughingstock of the nation, they stuck with senior running back Pete Van Valkenburg, a proven commodity who gained a school-record 1,386 yards and led the nation in rushing. Their first-string quarterback, Bill August, threw sixty-nine passes all season long, in 144 attempts, and had just two touchdown passes.

August graduated that season. His heir apparent was a senior-to-be named Dave Terry, a confident Californian with "BYU No. 1" on his personalized license plates and a good deal of enthusiasm for his ability to run the football team. Terry held onto the job in spring practice, when the eight-man quarterback convention convened daily. But by the end of the spring Sheide was second on the depth chart, and gaining.

There was only one thing missing. Sheide hadn't been injured yet, which was unusual. By August two-a-days that oversight was corrected. He pulled a groin during a practice scrimmage, and when the season opened in September in Cougar Stadium against Colorado State, he was on the sidelines — on crutches.

With Terry at quarterback, BYU lost that game, 21-13. In the season's second game, against Oregon State also in Cougar Stadium, Randy Litchfield was the starter and BYU rolled to a 37-14 win. Sheide was off his crutches and got in the game at the end to let the clock run out. His first pass in major college football came seconds later. He was supposed to hand off to the fullback, but he didn't. He faked the handoff, dropped back, spotted Sam Lobue behind the secondary, and hit him with a seventy-yard touchdown pass.

On the sideline, The Swamp Rat's eyes lit up.

For his final pass in a regular season major college game — against the University of Utah two seasons later — Sheide would also throw a touchdown pass. But that wasn't what made him unique. It was what he did in between.

Of course, no one was yet aware that he was the big fish in Provo, least of all Litchfield and Terry, who kept their one-two positions for one more week. For game three the Cougars traveled to Logan to play Utah State. It was a windy September day with gusts of up to thirty miles an hour. The score was 13-7 in favor of Utah State with just sixty-eight seconds left, at which point Sheide was sent into the game.

He completed six of ten passes on the final drive and moved the team seventy-five yards downfield against the wind. Unfortunately for the Cougars, they needed to go eighty yards for a touchdown. They and the clock expired on the five-yard line.

But Sheide had won the starting quarterback job at BYU — and all of Dewey Warren's experiments were about to be aired out.

The next week was homecoming at BYU, with a game against Iowa State. That day the 25,580 in attendance saw, for the first time, what the new passing game was all about. So did Iowa State. Matt Blair, the Cyclones' star monster back who would go on to play for the NFL's Minnesota Vikings, lined up across from Sheide all afternoon. He looked like a tourist on a Los Angeles freeway. He didn't know where to line up. He didn't know where to go.

Sometimes, neither did BYU. Delay-of-game penalties were common. Depending on where Iowa State set up defensively, the Cougars needed time at the line of scrimmage to call audibles. And since Blair and Company didn't know where they were going, time went quickly. If this was an historic occasion, it was also somewhat chaotic. Despite generating only 318 yards total offense, Iowa State hung on for a 26-24 win when BYU missed what would have been a game-winning field goal in the final seconds. Still, Sheide passed for 439 yards and three touchdowns on twenty-nine of forty-one completions.

"He ridiculed them," said The Swamp Rat, undeterred by the defeat.

The passing statistics were aberrational. They looked like a misprint. Something had gone right. The patient had lost but he hadn't died. Iowa State, like a lot of other teams in the next few years, left the field echoing the same line Butch Cassidy was saying to the Sundance Kid in the era's most popular Western: "Who *are* those guys?"

Looking back on it, a lot of people say that Gary Sheide had it lucky. He didn't have the pressure of coming along behind a Jim McMahon or a Gifford Nielsen, or a Johnny Unitas or a Terry Bradshaw, for that matter. He had nothing to prove at a school that had turned defeat into an art form. It wasn't Pass U. back then. What did he have to lose?

But what he did have to contend with was something none of his All-American successors would encounter. He had a half-century of ineptness riding on his right arm. He had moved in with a program that didn't know how to win. There were skeptics everywhere. In that sense, Sheide had more pressure than any of the others would ever have. Somebody had to get it started. Who better than a junior college transfer from California who had been detoured along his way to becoming a big-league shortstop? He hadn't had to endure any seasons at BYU when he wasn't playing regularly, when the mediocrity could pull him down. He was impervious to traditions and to pressures.

He wasn't a typical Mormon boy. He wasn't a Mormon boy, period. "I was an off-the-wall guy from California," said Sheide. "I don't know, maybe I needed them and maybe they needed me. It could be it was fate."

Whatever it was, after the Iowa State game it started to work.

Sheide and Warren agreed on the importance of the forward pass, but that didn't mean they didn't have their occasional differences of opinion. Neither was an introvert. They were both opinionated, and they were not that far apart in age (Sheide was twenty-one in 1975, The Swamp Rat was twenty-eight). And with the imperviousness of youth, they both second-guessed Edwards. A common scene in 1973 was Sheide and Warren huddled together during a time-out, trying to figure out what play would work. Edwards would poke his head in and make a suggestion, and neither Sheide nor Warren would even bother to look up.

Sheide did click, completely, with Jay Miller. A receiver who had been personally recruited by Edwards in 1972, Miller had been promised he would get the ball a lot if he became a Cougar, and that he would set records and become an All-American.

Even Edwards didn't think he'd do it by his second year.

Like Sheide, Miller started out subtly enough in 1973. He caught six passes in the opening game, six passes in the second game, and eight passes in the third game. But the secondaries hadn't seen anything yet. In Sheide's first start against Iowa State, Miller caught twelve passes. In the next seven games he caught sixty-eight more — giving him an even one hundred for the season.

In the first fifty years of Cougar football there had only been three seasons when the entire BYU football team had managed to catch one hundred passes.

Miller might have caught more except he was ejected from the Utah game — even Californians tended to get caught up in the emotion of that rivalry — and in the last game of the season he was rested early after his fifth reception of the game (and one hundredth overall).

20

That last game was in El Paso against UTEP. The night before the game Miller and Sheide were in their hotel room watching the sports on TV. The sportscaster detailed how the Miners planned to stop Sheide and Miller the next day in the Sun Bowl.

Now that they had their attention . . .

Sheide and Miller played barely a half each, Miller long enough to catch his century pass and Sheide long enough to complete seventeen of twenty-eight passes for 218 yards and one touchdown. BYU won 63-0.

Sheide ended the season ranked number three in the nation in total offense and number two in the nation in passing, with 17.7 completions per game at 60.2 percent accuracy. He was barely beaten out for the passing title by San Diego State's Jesse Freitas. The next season Sheide again sat down early in the final game, against Utah, and as a result lost the passing title to Cal-Berkeley's Steve Bartkowski—by one pass.

No matter. They were having fun now. After the Iowa State loss Sheide had led the 1973 Cougars to a 4-2 record. He had beaten Utah at Utah—and convincingly at that, with a four-touchdown-pass, 46-22 blowout in a Salt Lake City snowstorm. He had thrown twenty-two touchdown passes in just eight games while passing for a school-record 2,350 yards, and he had thrown just twelve interceptions. The Cougars scored 220 points in their final four games, and for their last trick they scored sixty-three points against UTEP, the second-highest, single-game total in BYU history.

Gary Sheide had brought instant and considerable credibility to the great passing experiment.

Then he returned to Antioch for the summer and did something he shouldn't have done. He played softball.

1974

He didn't play just a little softball on Saturday afternoon. The American Realty team in Antioch wanted Sheide's arm at short-stop, and they signed him for the season by offering him all the

21

innings he could play. He couldn't turn that down. It was a good move on American Realty's part. They finished second in the 1974 California state tournament. It was not a good move on Sheide's part. He didn't warm up before games, and he got a lot of work at shortstop. It was too much for his temperamental right arm. By the time he arrived back in Provo for his senior season, he had a severe tendonitis problem in his right shoulder — and an eleven-game football schedule that wouldn't wait.

Once the season was underway, he practiced sparingly. He told only Greg about the tendonitis, and he took cortisone pills he had acquired from the team doctor after bruising his ribs the year before in a game against Weber State.

The way the season started, it didn't matter. The Cougars went to Hawaii for the opener and, amid the distractions of Waikiki Beach, lost 15-13. Next they lost to Utah State 9-6, and then dropped a game to Iowa State 34-7. In that game — in sharp contrast to the year before — Sheide threw just eleven passes and completed only four. Something was obviously different, and it wasn't just Sheide's arm, which was in reasonably good shape for game days, just not the morning after.

The difference was a new coach. After the 1973 season Dewey Warren received a job offer from Kansas State. He looked at it as a promotion and took it. Edwards brought in Dwain Painter, who had been an assistant coach at the College of San Mateo, to coach the quarterbacks. Painter was more of a traditional coach. In spite of Warren's playbook, which Edwards gave him to use, Painter (who wondered if this was a football team or a circus aerial act) wanted the Cougars to run as much as they passed. He put in a lot of rollouts and option plays for the quarterback.

After the Iowa State game there was unrest about both Sheide as the quarterback and Edwards' passing system in general — which was trying to coexist with Painter's new balance.

Edwards called Sheide into his office.

"We're taking a lot of heat right now," Edwards said. He paused. If there was one thing LaVell Edwards was good at, besides organizing football teams, it was pausing. He could pause anytime, anywhere, between any words. He paused now. Sheide just stood there.

"Don't worry about it," said Edwards finally.

As Sheide was leaving, the coach told him something else. They were taking the rollouts and options out of the game plan. They were going back to the pocket. "If we're going to lose," said Edwards, "we might as well lose throwing."

The fourth game was the conference opener, at Colorado State in Ft. Collins. The Rams were favored. Sheide stayed in the pocket, completing eleven of fourteen passes for three touchdowns. As a psychological boost, the Cougars reactivated Jay Miller, who had been injured in August practices and hadn't yet played a down that season. It seemed to work. With fifteen seconds remaining Miller had two receptions and the Cougars had the ball and a 33-27 lead. And Colorado State was out of time-outs.

All Sheide had to do was fall on the ball and watch the clock tick off the final seconds.

Orrin Olsen, the BYU center, got over the ball and prepared to hike it. Kevin McLain, CSU's middle linebacker, looked at Olsen and, according to Sheide, who of course was standing extremely nearby, said, "I'm going to rip your [expletive deleted] head off!"

Olsen, apparently interested to see if McLain was going to follow through on his promise, looked up as he was centering the ball and only got it halfway to Sheide before it fell to the ground. The fumble was recovered by Colorado State at the BYU fifteen-yard line.

In one play the Rams quickly said thank you by scoring a touchdown. They could have then completely ruined BYU's evening with a game-winning extra point. But they celebrated too early and were penalized fifteen yards for running onto the field after the touchdown and setting a stadium record for high-fives. The twenty-five-yard, extra-point kick failed, and the game ended in a 33-33 tie.

BYU was still winless at 0-3-1, and depressed. But as it would turn out, a tie in the conference opener was like kissing Raquel

Welch. That missed kick was the only gift the Cougars would need.

In the next game, against Wyoming, Sheide threw more times than he had in the two previous games combined, and the Cougars won 38-7. Then they beat UTEP 45-21 on the strength of five Sheide touchdown passes. For his heroics Sheide was named UPI's national Back of the Week. Five more Sheide TD passes helped them beat Arizona 37-13 — no small feat considering Arizona was ranked fourteenth in the nation at the time. BYU had finally beat a "football school."

The nation was starting to take notice. Gary Sheide was being compared to Joe Namath, sloped shoulders and all. He even wore number 12, Namath's number. After the win over Arizona, BYU followed with wins over Air Force and Arizona State — a crucial 21-18 triumph in Provo that saw Sheide throw two touchdown passes to stop the Sun Devils' WAC championship string at five. At that point *Sports Illustrated* dispatched writer Ron Reid to the New Mexico game in Albuquerque. There Sheide threw two more touchdown passes before sitting down early in a 36-3 rout. The resulting story on BYU — "Oh What a BYUtiful Mourning . . . Given up for dead, Brigham Young is making a lively try for a title" — was the first full-scale article ever done on BYU football in a major national magazine.

In the season's final game BYU clinched its second-ever conference championship by scoring only its eighth win ever — and second straight — against Utah, this time with a 48-20 rout in Provo. The season that had started 0-3-1 had ended with seven straight victories. It was the longest winning streak in BYU football history. Sheide had thrown for 2,174 yards and twenty-three touchdowns while completing 181 of three hundred passes. In the last eight games he had thrown for twenty-two of those touchdowns and completed sixteen of 239 passes for 61.1 percent accuracy.

Two years earlier they had handed him a crash helmet and pointed him to the test car, and now he was emerging without a scratch. You could win with the pass if you had the right quarterback — that's what Gary Sheide told BYU.

Immediately after the Utah win the Fiesta Bowl called from

Tempe, Arizona, to invite Brigham Young to be in their bowl game on December 28, 1974. The Cougars said they thought they could make it.

FIESTA BOWL, 1974

Having never before had their team in a bowl game, BYU's fans responded accordingly. Their reaction was somewhere between Armistice Day and July 4th. Immediately after Christmas they packed into cars or chartered airplanes and made their way south, to Arizona. Provo was abandoned, as were parts of Salt Lake City. Gary Sheide and the Cougars had rearranged a lot of holiday plans with their date in Sun Devil Stadium against Oklahoma State.

In the days before the bowl game Sheide spent his time studying films of the Cowboys—which was how he came to the conclusion that they didn't have a notion about how to stop BYU's passing game. Only seventy-six passes had been completed, and 195 thrown, against OSU all season long in the run-oriented Big 8 Conference. Sheide's 181 completions in three hundred attempts was in another league entirely.

The tendonitis was still there, but Sheide had had almost a month's rest since the end of the season, and it wouldn't stop this game, nor would it stop him from going to Honolulu for the Hula Bowl.

As he passed the business manager's room in the hotel, Gary slipped in and picked up a sideline pass for Greg. He wanted his brother there to witness the execution.

Then came the kickoff and the two first-quarter drives that scored two quick field goals giving them the 6-0 lead. The Cougars had averaged thirty-four points per win in their seven-game streak to get this far. They were right on schedule.

But as Sheide was setting up the second field goal, he stepped in the pocket for a pass, clicked off his choices of receivers, made his delivery, and then went down as though he'd been shot. Phil Dokes, a 6'5", 256-pound sophomore defensive tackle who did not say please and thank you, had blindsided him from the right.

25

Sheide moved to get up. His elbow was locked and the wind was knocked out of him. First things first. He got his breath. Then he picked up his arm, and something snapped.

He was finished for the day, with a separated shoulder that wouldn't heal for a month. The Cougars were shut out the rest of the game and lost 16-6. Sheide flew home to Provo, the opposite direction from Honolulu. A quarterback from Southern Cal, Pat Haden, took his place in the Hula Bowl. He was named MVP and went high in the NFL draft.

Sheide didn't, as agent Weiner had predicted, go high in the NFL draft. His number-three selection had been a prediction based on undamaged goods. Sheide wound up as the first player drafted in the third round, by the Cincinnati Bengals. Greg was his agent.

At Cincinnati's training camp, Sheide was mending from the shoulder separation, and he still had the tendonitis. If anything, it had gotten worse. He bluffed his way through practices and made it past the final cut. In the last preseason scrimmage the Bengals put him in to see what he could do against the Washington Redskins. He was his old phenomenal self, completing seventeen of eighteen passes. But the next day when coach Paul Brown asked him to throw, he couldn't pass the ball more than thirty yards.

When they waived him, Sheide had one question. Could anyone point him in the direction of the nearest fishing stream?

GIFFORD NIELSEN

"THE ROOTS OF MY RAISING RUN DEEP"
—*Merle Haggard, 1976*

*W*illie Scroggins, a 6'5", 226-pound defensive end for the Arizona State Sun Devils, did not like quarterbacks. And, as reel after reel in the Arizona State film room verified, quarterbacks didn't think much of Willie Scroggins, either. He was the star of the film room. His teammates would cheer as Scroggins sacked quarterback after quarterback. They said he took out more quarterbacks than the homecoming queen. He was a highlight film all by himself.

The first time Gifford Nielsen played a minute of major college football, Willie Scroggins was the welcoming committee.

It was the third game of the season in the fall of 1975. Arizona State had the best football team in the school's history, a team that was on its way to a perfect 12-0 season and a number-two national ranking. At the moment the Sun Devils had the BYU Cougars right where they wanted them: deep in the heart of Sun Devil Stadium with nowhere to go. Entering the fourth quarter the score was 7-0, ASU. Under the circumstances, a commanding lead. Scroggins and the rest of the ASU defense had the Cougars stuck in reverse. Mark Giles, BYU's starting quarterback, was not making a strong Heisman Trophy push.

Nielsen, a sophomore, was Giles' backup. Before the game he was told by LaVell Edwards to be prepared to see some playing time if Giles didn't generate any offense. The Cougars hadn't made the covers of any football magazines after scoring just twenty-one and seventeen points in the first two games of the season, both losses, to Bowling Green and Colorado State, respectively. Now they weren't scoring at all.

Edwards unfolded his arms and nodded at Nielsen.

Sun Devil Stadium had recently been expanded, and 50,944 fans were crowded into their seats. But as he walked to the middle of the field Nielsen didn't notice any of them. He had watched the game films, too. Willie Scroggins had his full and undivided attention.

In the next six minutes, Nielsen threw eleven passes, completed just four, had another intercepted, was sacked three times for a net loss of sixty-one yards, and, finally, as advertised in his own mind, met Willie Scroggins head-on and was knocked semiunconscious and carried off the field.

He had made the Arizona State highlight film.

PROVO, UTAH
1954-1972

From the beginning, Gifford Nielsen had it all — except he wasn't very fast. But then, he didn't need to be. He had five sisters.

The youngest of the five, Laurie, was three when Gifford was born. Nancy, Julie, Shirley, Peggy, and Laurie mothered him like a puppy; and Gifford, in the process, became a sort of modern Tom Sawyer. His sisters would do anything for him, from drying the dishes to cleaning up his room, and he would let them. A team player from the start.

If five sisters weren't enough, there were always the forty or so college students who shared the Nielsen house on 1280 Cherry Lane in Provo. When Gifford was six months old, Stan and Lois Nielsen turned their home into a boarding house for BYU students. They provided morning and evening meals and sleeping rooms in the basement, and built a dumbwaiter to send the meals downstairs. In the society of student boarding houses, Maniac Manor, as it came to be known, gained something of a five-star reputation. There was always a waiting list to get in. The Manor adopted hundreds of students every year, who in turn adopted Gifford, the kid with a thousand siblings.

Gifford's parents worked full-time. Stan Nielsen was a department manager at Bennett Paint and Glass in Provo and, later, a salesman for Granite Furniture; Lois Nielsen was a nurse. But if Stan and Lois weren't home a lot, there was always someone in the boarding house to play catch with; and, outside, Cherry Lane in the sixties had an abundance of kids. Gifford's best friend, Jeff Smith, lived next door. Their yards were joined together by the basketball hoop in the Smith's backyard.

In this existence, Gifford Nielsen grew up without complaint. He woke up like kids did in Disney movies. "Gee, isn't this going to be a great day?" was his standard opening line. He had everything but adversity.

He was something straight out of *Parents* magazine. He was polite. He was friendly. He went to church. At school he was the teacher's favorite. He became a kind of children's Father Flanagan. When he chose up sides for a game of football or baseball, he took the kids first who usually went last. When fights started on the playground, he broke them up.

He might have been too much to take, a goody-goody castigated for life, except for two major factors in his favor: He was a very good athlete whose teams always seemed to win; and just about anybody could beat him in a race, which tended to keep him human.

He wasn't what you'd call well rounded. His three favorite

things were sports, sports, and sports. In the American sports explosion of the 1960s, when television and the NFL and the NBA were coming into their own, Gifford Nielsen rode the lead wave. He did not study music or great literature. He didn't know a Picasso from a Rembrandt. He did not yearn to visit European cultures or explore the theory of relativity. He was not interested in cars or guns or science fiction. He was not an Eagle Scout. He got good grades in school, but he didn't study with a passion. He played sports with a passion. He was the kind of kid who taped himself before playing football in the street. He daubed shoe polish below his eyes before he played baseball in the backyard. He wore a jersey when he shot baskets in the driveway.

He was a member of the Provo Downtown Coaches Club when he was thirteen. He went to the meetings to listen to the BYU coaches. His parents had two season tickets to the BYU basketball games, and he had more ways to connive his mother out of her ticket than he had ways of getting his sisters to vacuum his room. Lois Nielsen rarely saw a game. When she did go to the games, played in the Smith Fieldhouse, Gifford volunteered as a ball boy for the visiting team or sold popcorn—anything to get in the door.

Growing up like that, raised on sports on Cherry Lane in Provo surrounded always by BYU students and in the shadow of Y Mountain, Stanley Gifford Nielsen—the Stanley was after his dad, the Gifford after his maternal grandfather, A. L. Gifford, and for some reason Gifford stuck—became a BYU disciple. He would play basketball for the Cougars one day, he was sure of that.

That basketball would be his first love was understandable. Stan Nielsen had played basketball at BYU, as a 6'4" guard for coach Eddie Kimball from 1940-41. Before that he'd been an all-conference guard at Snow College in Ephraim, Utah, and had coached high school basketball for two seasons. In addition to having this basketball heredity, Gifford grew up in Provo, where basketball in the fifties and sixties had become a sort of second religion. Provo High School had the premier program in the state. The Provo city leagues were well established, starting as low as the fifth grade. And at BYU, under Stan Watts, the Cougars rarely had a bad team. They won the NIT in 1951 and 1966. In 1972—

the year Gifford was a high school senior — they built the biggest on-campus basketball arena in America, the Marriott Center. And filled it every game. That year's Cougar team was ranked in the top ten in the country.

But in the early years Gifford didn't have to specialize with basketball, so he didn't. There was a sport for every season; and while he wasn't particularly fast, he was bigger and taller than the other kids his age and he was a prolific winner. He was an all-star in Little League baseball as a pitcher and a shortstop. He was on the fifth-grade city league basketball team that won the sixth-grade championship, and on the sixth-grade team that won the seventh-grade championship. In junior high his parents moved out of Maniac Manor and into a home next to Riverside Country Club, and he became a low-handicap golfer.

He was on city league flag football teams that won their division every year from the fourth through ninth grades. Tackle football was the only sport in which he had no early formal training. Not until Gifford got to Provo High in the tenth grade did he put on a helmet and pads. In his first organized game of tackle football he was a member of the Provo High sophomore team of 1970 that traveled to American Fork for a game against kids who had grown up in organized youth tackle leagues.

On the first play of the game, with Nielsen at quarterback and his buddy Jeff Smith at wide receiver, Gifford dropped back and threw Smith a sixty-yard touchdown pass.

This was going to be easy.

When the dust settled two hours later, American Fork had won, 56-6.

It was not long, however, before Nielsen and his teammates got the hang of playing in pads. They lost their next game as sophomores, and that was it — they didn't lose again the rest of the season. Then, as juniors on the varsity, they pulled off something highly unusual: They beat Orem High School.

For almost as long as Gifford had been alive, Orem High had beaten Provo High in football. Going into the 1971 game, the streak was at thirteen. In spite of the lopsided nature of the series, interest was still high and the game was moved from Provo High's field to the BYU Stadium to accommodate the crowd. Dick Hill, the Provo coach, held a chalk talk with his players before the game. He mentioned Orem's winning streak with trepidation.

"Don't worry," Nielsen said to Hill. "I've never lost to Orem."

Then he went out and threw a tackle-eligible pass to Kelly Harris, a future BYU teammate, for the winning touchdown.

"He was a player's player," said Hill. "He always called his own plays. I'd just give him the game. You could feel inferior as a coach, coaching Gifford Nielsen."

After beating Orem, Hill retired a contented coach and Bry Lake took over as Provo High's football coach for Gifford's senior season. Lake switched to the wishbone offense, a peculiar move considering his quarterback's slowness afoot. Provo struggled early in the season, losing to Judge Memorial and Kearns. But then the team caught on to the wishbone and went all the way to the Class 4-A state championship game, where the Bulldogs had a rematch with Kearns. Kearns scored in the last two minutes for a 28-21 win in BYU Stadium.

Little did anyone know that it would be the last, and only, game Gifford would ever lose in that stadium.

It would also be the last game he would ever lose in high school. Gifford moved immediately into the basketball season, and Provo High won thirty-four straight games and the state championship. Included in the wins were three over Orem High, two during the regular season played in front of more than twelve thousand fans each in the Marriott Center, and one in the Utah state championship game at the University of Utah Special Events Center.

Nielsen was named MVP of the 4-A classification and was a consensus all-state basketball player. If he wasn't on top of the basketball world, at least in Utah, who was? For icing, at the previous summer's Cougar basketball camp—he'd been attending since he was eleven—he had been the camp one-on-one champion.

His apprenticeship was over. He had prepped in the Provo City youth basketball programs and won titles every year. He had won the state championship at Provo High. He had never lost to Orem High. He had sat at the feet of the Cougars in the Smith

Fieldhouse and the Marriott Center. He didn't care if they knew of his exploits in North Carolina or Los Angeles or Indiana. He just wanted them to know across the street. He was now ready to go to BYU, and study basketball.

There was one hitch.

BYU didn't want him.

1973-1974

It wasn't that the coaches at BYU didn't like Gifford Nielsen. Everybody *liked* Gifford Nielsen. He helped little old ladies across the street, and he wasn't into drugs or long hair, and he said "sir" and "ma'am." They would let their daughters date him, no problem. But as far as his potential as a major college athlete was concerned, they had their doubts. He was not fast. He was not particularly agile and, for basketball, he was at an in-between height. Six-feet-five-inches was fine if you were Oscar Robertson or Julius Erving, if you could jump out of the gym; or it was fine if you were Bob Cousy, looking for your next assist. Nielsen was hard-nosed and he could shoot, but that was about it.

In football his physical skills were not overpowering, either. He was not muscular. He had fair skin and a baby face. He didn't have a strong passing arm, and when he was clocked in the forty-yard dash they were always checking the watch to see why it hadn't shut off.

It's hard to give a scholarship based on a sixth sense and a competitive spirit, which is what Gifford really had going for him. Those were the intangibles that were always getting him places he shouldn't have otherwise been. He was at his best when he was creating. He had a sense that extended beyond his peripheral vision. He could size up defenses in a matter of seconds and, like a chess player, see several moves in advance. In that sense he was made to be a quarterback, although no one, including Gifford, knew it in 1973 when he was coming out of Provo High and the coaches at BYU were trying to figure out how to tell the most popular kid in town that they weren't sure he could cut it. Eddie

Kimball was one who did know that Gifford should be a quarterback. The former BYU football and basketball coach, who had coached Gifford's father in basketball, saw Lois Nielsen one day in a local market. "That boy of yours is going to be some football player," Kimball said.

But in 1973 Eddie Kimball was retired.

The Cougars had used subtleness in an effort to let Gifford know where he stood. They typically designated their top local basketball recruits by giving them tickets to the games on campus. Several of Gifford's teammates at Provo High got the tickets regularly. He never did. To see the games he had to use his mother's ticket.

Not only was he without honor in his own county, he wasn't heavily recruited elsewhere. The University of Utah offered him a football scholarship, and Utah State University offered him a basketball scholarship. He got an offer from the Naval Academy in Annapolis to become an officer and a gentleman and play on the basketball team.

Nielsen dismissed them all. He wanted to be a Cougar. He considered it his destiny.

He also had some clout.

He had been a member in long-standing of the Downtown Coaches Club. And Stan Nielsen did happen to be the current president of the club. And they did have a lot of friends around town.

Recruiting sometimes gets political. The recruiting of Gifford Nielsen got political. A number of influential businessmen — i. e., people who buy season tickets and advertisements in the game programs and donate generously to the booster club fund — thought Gifford was destined to be a Cougar as much as he thought he was destined to be a Cougar.

In the athletic office at BYU they considered all of the above and called a meeting with Glenn Potter, the new basketball coach, and LaVell Edwards, the new football coach, and came to a compromise.

They would give Gifford Nielsen a half-ride scholarship in

basketball and a half-ride scholarship in football, and would leave it up to him to decide which sport he wanted to play.

English translation: Neither sport wanted him.

As a BYU freshman in the fall of 1973 Nielsen reported to football practice. But when the middle of October—and the first day of basketball practice—came along, he was gone. A lot of people thought for good, especially when a month later he was starting for the varsity.

His first football season had also been Gary Sheide's first. Quarterback coach Dewey Warren and Sheide hadn't yet started to show what they had in mind with the passing game. Nielsen was curious about the new playbook, and he took to Warren's system with enthusiasm in running the freshman team. As the freshman starter at quarterback he directed the team to a 4-0 record. But this was 1973, when the term *stadium expansion* meant turning it into a dairy farm. Gifford Nielsen didn't want to be the next Gary Sheide, he wanted to be the next Kresimir Cosic.

The first day of basketball practice he took an elbow to the face from Dave Checketts, a freshman walk-on from Bountiful who would go on to become the president of the Utah Jazz. Nielsen had to have stitches and was out for a week. So much for the noncontact sport. In football, he hadn't missed a day.

When he came back it took him less than a week to be promoted off the freshman team to the varsity.

This was both good news and bad. When a major college basketball team plays a freshman it either means he's Magic Johnson or Larry Bird, or it means the varsity is in serious trouble.

The 1973-74 BYU varsity basketball team was in serious trouble. Glenn Potter was in his second year as head coach and was feeling not unlike a broker on Wall Street in 1929. In 1972 he had inherited one of the best basketball programs in the country. Stan Watts had retired after coaching for twenty-three years and had left Potter an All-American in Kresimir Cosic and the new Marriott Center to play in. Yet Potter's first team had gone a disappointing 19-7 and failed to either win the WAC or qualify for the NCAA tournament. Now Cosic had graduated and Potter's conservative slowdown offense—in sharp contrast to the crowd-pleasing, fast-break style used by Watts—was being soundly criticized.

Nielsen was called on, as a freshman, to plug his finger in the dike. Midway through the season, with the team struggling with a 6-7 record, he was named a starter prior to the Utah game in Salt Lake City. More good news, bad news. His defensive assignment was Luther "Ticky" Burden, the Utes' leading scorer. Utah won 104-86, but Potter thought Nielsen, who scored four points, did an "adequate" job on Burden by holding him to twenty-nine. Nielsen started most of the games for the rest of the season, especially when the other team had a high scorer who needed to be guarded somewhat, well, physically. Nielsen covered Arizona State's Lionel Hollins and Arizona's Coniel Norman, among others. Gifford Nielsen was basketball's answer to Willie Scroggins. He felt like a professional hit man. His scoring average was 3.5 points a game, but he led the league in sacks.

For rest and relaxation he reported to spring football.

He wasn't the only quarterback on the squad. Sheide had emerged as the starter, and he was surrounded by understudies. Edwards asked Nielsen to consider a redshirt year. Nielsen agreed and worked out with the team in both the spring and the fall as a player on hold. The next October he was back to basketball, this time as a full-time starter. If nothing else, BYU was getting its money's worth.

The basketball team had gone 11-15 during Nielsen's freshman year—only the second losing season in Provo in eleven years—and in 1974-75 the team didn't fare much better. The Cougars improved one game, to 12-14, and lost to Utah twice. A swingman, Nielsen continued to consistently draw tough defensive assignments but increased his scoring average to 8.5 points per game. In the last game of the season, during a 91-82 loss at Colorado State, he hit a career high twenty-four points. He suddenly had new hope. Rumors were out that Potter would be fired—he was—and with a new coaching change would come new possibilities. It could mean a new beginning.

But when Frank Arnold was hired from UCLA and moved

into the Marriott Center as BYU's new head coach, his reaction wasn't what Nielsen had hoped it would be.

"Oh, do you play basketball?" Arnold said.

Nielsen needed to be believed in. He had always thrived when he was in a positive atmosphere, when he could be loose to use his wile and wits. He had flourished that way at Provo High. But if his creativity was limited, he had no edge.

In the spring of 1975 he had no edge.

He married Wendy Olsen, the only steady girlfriend he'd ever had, in April. They had gone through school together, from Wasatch Elementary on. She was a cheerleader at Provo High and at BYU. She married the quarterback. The storybook life continued—except now the quarterback didn't know what he was going to do.

Frank Arnold wasn't excited about him. Neither was Dwain Painter, the quarterback coach. LaVell Edwards was undecided. Gifford was doing what he'd always wanted to do. He was playing basketball for BYU. But the Cougars were getting drilled in the process. And the basketball coach was telling him that, at 6'5", wouldn't he have a great view looking over the offensive line.

He determined that a change of majors might be in his best interest.

1975

Willie Scroggins had made him think otherwise.

It wasn't just Scroggins and the disastrous first start at Arizona State. As he flew home from Phoenix, Nielsen reflected on his first six months as a full-time football player. You might have called it an inauspicious beginning, but that would have been quite an understatement.

In the spring, Giles, a senior with a good arm and Sheide's backup the year before, was the front-runner. But with an asterisk. After taking over for Sheide in the Fiesta Bowl, he had failed to produce any points in BYU's 16-6 loss to Oklahoma State.

But neither Nielsen nor Jeff Duva, another top contender,

had given Giles much cause for worry. At the end of spring practice Painter considered Giles the best candidate to run the revised offense the Cougars were turning to now that Sheide had graduated. Slowly but surely, Painter was steering BYU away from the passing game Dewey Warren had set up. He was moving again toward a balanced attack, half runs and half passes. He set up counter plays and option plays for the quarterbacks, as well as sprint draws and, more radical yet, basic running plays.

Wind sprints were never Nielsen's strong point. In spring practice he wowed no one. He edged out Duva for the number-two spot on the depth chart, and by the end of August two-a-days he was still number two — but not convincingly.

Now, flying back from the loss at ASU, after getting his chance and blowing it, he was nursing a Willie Scroggins hangover and pondering the meaning of life. He had left basketball behind, he had not had a good spring, and he had been carried off the field at Arizona State. Surely Edwards was not thinking this was the quarterback around which to build his offense. And by Monday morning it could get worse. He could be third string.

They listed the depth chart early every Monday on the training room wall. All day Sunday, Nielsen hoped against hope. He felt like he had as a seventh-grader at Farrer Junior High School the day they posted the cut list for the basketball team. He was the first person to the training room Monday morning.

He was third string.

After that came the period where no one talks to you. When you've just been demoted to third string, people do anything to avert your gaze.

Nielsen quietly took over as the scout-team quarterback. For the week his assignment was to imitate that week's opposing quarterback, New Mexico's Steve Myer, a senior who would rank number two in passing and number three in total offense that year in the nation. Nielsen used his imagination. He *was* Myer and his receivers were all Preston Dennard, the New Mexico wide receiver who was Myer's favorite target and who would rank third in the country in pass receptions that season. He kept the scout-team receivers after practice every day. He worked overtime. He hoped that some way, someday, he'd get another chance.

Meanwhile, the Cougar coaches were hoping he wouldn't. It is not especially comfortable to have a quarterback on the team who has fallen out of favor. Tom Baltzer, a former BYU player and at the time a graduate assistant coach, was married to Gifford's sister, Shirley. As Gifford's brother-in-law, he was elected to have a talk with Frank Arnold to see if the basketball team might be interested in taking back Nielsen's scholarship once basketball practice started in two weeks.

In the meantime came the next game.

Because it was General Conference weekend for the Mormon Church, the fourth game of the season, versus the New Mexico Lobos, was played on Friday night. The thirty thousand seats in Cougar Stadium were about two-thirds filled to see if the 0-3 Cougars had any prayers left. It soon appeared they didn't. Myer threw a touchdown pass to Gil Stewart, and the Lobos added a safety and field goal. Late in the third quarter they held a 12-0 lead.

By this time Duva was at quarterback. Giles, who didn't like to wear hip pads, had been taken out early by a hip-pointer. Duva threw twenty passes and completed only five. The Cougars were working on seven straight quarters of scoreless football.

Edwards looked at Gifford. "Giff had never done a thing, in practice or anywhere else, to give us confidence in him," said Edwards later.

But the coach was out of options. He sent him into the game anyway.

Nielsen felt oddly relaxed.

His first play was a nineteen-yard completion to Jeff Nilsson. His second play was a six-yard run on an option. On his third play the Lobos came hard with a safety blitz. "I was looking at this guy staring me down. He's got fire in his eyes," said Nielsen. So he sidestepped him and tossed a five-yard pass to running back Dave Lowry, who went thirty-seven yards for a touchdown.

"This is more like it," Nielsen said to himself as he trotted off the field.

New Mexico scored another field goal on its next possession, giving the Lobos a 15-7 lead. There was 11:47 remaining in the game. Nielsen came back in. The Cougars marched to the Lobo twenty-nine-yard line. Players were starting to talk in the huddle about what would work and who was open. "Throw the throw-back," said running back Jeff Blanc. "I'll streak down the side for a touchdown."

Nielsen did. And Blanc did.

The two-point conversion that would have tied the game failed. It was Nielsen's first incomplete pass of the night. But with 7:09 remaining the Cougars got the ball back on their own thirty-six-yard line. They put together a fourteen-play drive that got them to the fourteen-yard line with 1:48 to play. Edwards sent in Dave Taylor, the kicker, who made a thirty-yard field goal to give BYU a 16-15 win.

Nielsen had completed ten of twelve passes for 148 yards and two touchdowns, in the process setting a WAC record for best completion percentage in a game. Furthermore, he'd given BYU its first win of the season. And, most significantly, he had revived the pass at BYU. He had jump-started an offense that had stalled since Gary Sheide's departure. He had saved it from an early demise. It was a wonderful life again.

Except for one detail. Dwain Painter didn't want Nielsen to start the next week against Air Force.

Nielsen and Edwards were guests on Edwards' KSL-TV coach's show the day after the New Mexico game. "Not everybody wants me to start you," the coach told Nielsen on their drive to Salt Lake City to tape the show. He paused.

"But I'm going to start you anyway."

In their coaches' meeting, when Painter lobbied hard for Giles, who he said shouldn't lose his starting job because of an injury, Edwards said, "I might have been a single-wing center, but I'm not that stupid. Here's a local kid who at least has done something. The other guys haven't done anything. We'll go with Gifford."

With his coach's confidence, Nielsen became a new football player. The Air Force game was BYU's centennial game, celebrating the school's one hundredth year. The atmosphere was the same as in the New Mexico game. BYU won 28-14 as Nielsen passed for 229 yards and a touchdown on fourteen of nineteen passing. He had no great affection for the option plays Painter kept sending in, so he changed a lot of them. The atmosphere in the huddle perked up. Success was infectious.

Through the next five games BYU lost only once, to Arizona, 36-20, and even then Nielsen had his best day as a passer, completing twenty-seven of forty-four passes for 387 yards. The Cougars were undefeated in the state of Utah—a feat that had occurred only twice before in history (1958 and 1966). They beat the University of Utah 51-20 and Utah State 24-7.

In the final game of the season, in a gesture to Giles, who was a senior, the coaches started Giles at Southern Mississippi. BYU lost 42-14 but still salvaged, at 6-5, a winning season. In the last eight games they had gone 6-2. For the year Nielsen completed 110 passes in 180 attempts for ten touchdowns and a .611 completion percentage that erased from the WAC record book the .603 Gary Sheide had set in 1973.

In the off-season Nielsen was in the Smith Fieldhouse annex throwing passes. Edwards walked by with a stranger.

"This is Doug Scovil," said Edwards. "He's with the San Francisco 49ers. He's going to be our new offensive coordinator."

Scovil looked at Nielsen.

"Son," he said, "we're going to turn you into a quarterback."

As Scovil walked away Nielsen said to himself, "I thought I already was one."

1976

Doug Scovil was out of work in the winter of 1976, which, considering his chosen profession, was nothing unusual. Football coaches change jobs as often as U.S. Cabinet secretaries and South American dictators. Scovil had been the special teams and offensive backfield coach for head coach Dick Nolan of the San Francisco 49ers, and when the 49ers decided they could live without Nolan they also decided they could live without his staff. Now

Scovil, forty-nine years old and a football coach all his adult life, was thinking he'd take some private business offers and get out of the game. Then the phone rang. It was Bill Walsh, soon to be the 49ers head coach and at the time the offensive coordinator for the San Diego Chargers. "There's an opening at BYU," Walsh told Scovil. "They're looking for an offensive coordinator."

Which was all Doug Scovil needed to hear. Thinking about getting out of coaching and getting out of coaching are different things entirely. If there was one job Scovil wanted it was offensive coordinator. If the next ship went down he at least wanted to be steering. In addition to that, he had a lot of ideas he was anxious to try, most of them having to do with the forward pass.

Dr. Frankenstein needed a laboratory. By taking a job offer at UCLA, Dwain Painter—who had not been entirely happy at a school that passed all the time—had opened one up at BYU.

Scovil called LaVell Edwards, whom he had never met, and used Bill Walsh as a reference. Their subsequent meeting went well. Edwards handed Scovil a copy of BYU's playbook and asked, "Well, what do you think?" Scovil replied, "I'd like to change most of it." Edwards tossed him a pencil.

Scovil agreed with what Dewey Warren had started. With a new playbook he wanted to expand all the concepts.

He didn't want to pass less. He wanted to pass more.

He set up more of a pro-set offense. Whenever possible, he wanted five receivers in patterns, including two running backs. He wanted to hit the short passes all the time to set up the deep patterns. His philosophy was to take what the defense gave up, and by doing so turn whatever decision the defense made into a wrong one. The passing game could exploit any defense. There was always a seam open, the trick was to find it.

It couldn't cure cancer or clear up the national debt, but Scovil believed that a disciplined, well-defined passing game could stop any legal defense known to man.

A college quarterback himself at the University of Pacific, and Roger Staubach's quarterback coach at the Naval Academy when Staubach won the Heisman Trophy in 1963, Scovil believed the passing game started and stopped with the quarterback. After looking at films of Nielsen, and after watching him in person, he told him, "If you'll just do what I tell you, you can be the Great Giff." Which was exactly what the Great Giff wanted to hear.

They became inseparable, the lean, pass-happy coach and the tall, fair-haired quarterback.

The first thing Scovil did was take movies — of Nielsen's feet.

There are those people who can walk into, say, a living room and, instead of just taking in the scene in general, notice if the magazines are lined up or if the pictures are crooked. Doug Scovil was like that. A detail man. A perfectionist. Wide receivers run exact routes, and quarterbacks don't move an inch from where they're supposed to. There is no place for false steps.

Scovil filmed Nielsen from the waist down and pointed out what his feet were doing wrong. He taught him an exact drop-back, with no wasted motion. It was the first time Nielsen had even considered working with his feet. He thought, "Okay, he's taught me the drop, now we can move on to something else." But for the rest of his playing days at BYU, he worked on drops for at least fifteen minutes at the start of every practice.

They were together constantly on the practice field. In the movie *Chariots of Fire* there is a scene where Sam Mussabini, the track coach, puts a stopwatch on Harald Abrahams, the British sprinter, and tells him, "I can get you two more steps." That was Doug Scovil and Gifford Nielsen.

Scovil and Nielsen met daily during the season, for at least an hour, whenever Nielsen could fit it into his class schedule. It was a practice Scovil would use with all the starting quarterbacks he coached at BYU.

But it wasn't everyone who could get into Scovil's office. He kept his desk locked at all times. His game plans had tighter security than national trade secrets. He could be as eccentric as he was innovative. Sometimes he wouldn't share his ideas with others on the coaching staff. Edwards, the consummate delegator of authority, didn't mind. At least not in the early years. Later on, after Scovil had come and gone twice and had become a coach in demand, egos would get in the way and they would have their differences. But not in 1976, when they were all probing the edge of the envelope.

Scovil could adapt anything to football. Nielsen was talking to him one day about the Mormon Church and told him about the Church's food storage program of keeping cracked wheat and other food on hand in case of emergency. The next day Scovil told the team, "We're going to have these plays in the back room that we'll only pull out for emergencies — like the cracked wheat."

One of those "cracked wheat" plays would win the 1980 Holiday Bowl when BYU beat Southern Methodist 46-45 on the last play of the game.

When Nielsen started his junior season in 1976 he was ready to put the gospel according to Doug Scovil to the test.

He was stunned when, in the opener at Kansas State, nothing worked in a 13-3 loss to the lightly regarded Wildcats. Nielsen threw two interceptions and no touchdowns.

"Don't worry," said Scovil as he and Nielsen left the field. "You'll see it."

The next game, against Colorado State in Provo, he saw it.

He threw four touchdown passes, and the Cougars won 42-18. The seams suddenly opened up. CSU had a defense loaded with pass rushers, future pros Bubba Baker and Mike Bell among them. "These guys want you," Scovil told Nielsen, which came as no surprise. "And they're not bad. So use it to your advantage. Work on your cadence, change it up, throw them off." With visions of Willie Scroggins in his head, Nielsen did just that. In the huddle he would call for the snap on the third "hut" and then, while calling out the count, say *"hut"* extra loud on two. After some early offsides calls, Baker and Bell were sufficiently frustrated. They never touched him.

Now all the new passing model needed was a final exam. It got it the next week in Tucson, Arizona. The University of Arizona had a football program that had emerged under coach Jim Young as one of the best in the West. The Wildcats had either won the WAC title or placed second for three seasons running while compiling a 26-7 record.

Against the Cougars, Arizona came up with a particularly

effective pass defense. On the day of the game Tucson was deluged by a rainstorm.

It was not a good day for flying.

The teams sloshed their way to a 16-16 tie, and it looked as though that would be that when, after an Arizona punt, there were fourteen seconds showing on the clock. BYU had the ball on the Arizona forty-three-yard line. There was time for one play. It didn't take a genius to know what was coming. Arizona's linebackers and defensive backs were already backing up when the Cougars broke their huddle.

When Nielsen got the snap from center the ball felt more like a medicine ball, heavy and wet and as passable as a bad check. He slipped his way to the right side of the pocket. His primary receiver was going deep, but he was covered. His secondary receiver, George Harris, was reversing his field, coming back across the center. He caught Nielsen's eye. Nielsen motioned. Harris turned upfield, a lunge ahead of his defender. Nielsen got a grip on the ball. With the release he thought there was no way he had thrown it far enough. But through the raindrops he watched the flight of the spiral.

The ball and Harris converged in the end zone with three seconds left on the clock.

"I couldn't believe it, George couldn't believe it," said Nielsen. But the fact was that BYU had a major road win, 23-16, and the forward pass had new respect. It had finally won in Arizona.

There was one more hurdle to worry about. In just three weeks, this time in Provo, Willie Scroggins and Gifford Nielsen were to have their second date.

On November 6, 1976, Arizona State and Willie Scroggins came to Provo, surprised to find that the rookie they'd last seen leaving Sun Devil field on a stretcher was now the top gun in a 5-2 program that had just whipped Southern Mississippi 63-19 and Utah State 45-14. Not that Arizona State was unnerved. Under coach Frank Kush the Sun Devils had won six of the last seven WAC titles and were perennially nationally ranked. They *owned* BYU. Dating back to 1949 they were 16-1 against the Cougars.

45

Gary Sheide's 21-18 win in 1974 in Provo had been the Cougars' only win.

Scovil's game plan for ASU, a team notoriously good at zone pass defense and suspect at man-to-man coverage, was to flood double movement into the zones, forcing the Sun Devils into playing man.

ASU took a 21-17 first-quarter lead, but BYU had set up the Sun Devils where they wanted them. The Cougars cruised to a 43-21 win. Kush spent the afternoon screaming at his defensive backs. "There was this weak safety," said Nielsen, "who always had about three people to cover. Kush kept railing on him on the sidelines, but there wasn't anything he could do. We had four options on every pass, depending on how they rotated."

Scroggins, bigger and stronger than a year ago, and as prejudiced as ever against quarterbacks, could see Nielsen; but he couldn't touch him. BYU's line was blocking better, and Nielsen wasn't taking any false steps. Scroggins did manage to grab Nielsen by his right shoulder early in the second quarter and was all set to give him another tackle he'd remember, or wouldn't remember, when Nielsen flipped the ball to his left hand and threw a pass. Scroggins had to let him go. For the game he was credited with just two tackles and no sacks.

After that game, after the Cougars had swept the Arizona schools and accumulated a 6-2 record, after scoring 151 points in their last three games, Brigham Young University broke into the national rankings. In the United Press International poll of November 9, 1976, the Cougars were ranked nineteenth in the nation.

And they were no one-week wonder. To stay ranked is easy. Just keep winning. The Cougars kept winning. They beat UTEP 40-27 as Nielsen threw four touchdown passes for 319 yards. They beat New Mexico 21-8, and he threw three more. Then he threw three more to beat the University of Utah in Salt Lake City and close out the regular season with a 9-2 record and the WAC championship. In all, Nielsen had thrown twenty-nine touchdown passes for 3,192 yards and had completed 207 passes in 372 attempts.

A lot had happened in college football since Rutgers played Princeton in the first game in 1869, and there wasn't much new every year. But this story was. A perennial loser in the Rocky Mountains had climbed into the nation's top twenty by using the forward pass; and the quarterback was a hometown hero who didn't drink, smoke or cuss and who had been third-string four games into the season. Members of the national media couldn't have been more interested if they'd uncovered a drug scandal. Nielsen was invited to New York City, where he made a tour of the newspapers and radio stations. He became an instant Heisman Trophy candidate — finishing sixth in that year's voting after coming from nowhere — and was named a first-team All-American by the Football Writers Association.

In Provo he was in heavy demand. They asked him to speak to the Downtown Coaches Club. Church and civic groups were after him. The Osmond Brothers, who weren't aware Nielsen was married, called and asked if he wanted a date with Marie.

BYU went to a bowl game that December for only the second time in its history, and the first time as an at-large invitee. The Tangerine Bowl (later the Florida Citrus Bowl) in Orlando, Florida, arranged for a rematch between the teams that had met in the 1974 Fiesta Bowl — Oklahoma State and BYU.

The Cowboys had virtually the same team as two years before, and they were that much improved. They had gone 8-3 during the regular season and had beaten Oklahoma 31-24. Only Nebraska and Missouri managed to beat them in the Big 8 Conference, and barely at that. Nebraska won 14-10, and Missouri 20-19. OSU still had Phil Dokes, the defensive tackle who had taken Gary Sheide out in the Fiesta Bowl, and they had junior running back Terry Miller, who finished fourth that year in the Heisman Trophy voting. The 1976 Tangerine Bowl was a lopsided game. BYU scored twenty-one points. Oklahoma State scored forty-nine.

As good as it had become in twelve games, the BYU passing game still had room for improvement. That was fine with Doug Scovil and Gifford Nielsen. They weren't going anywhere.

47

1977

Gifford Nielsen bought a new suit for the annual ABC-TV anti-drug, ratings-hype, college football tour in the summer of 1977. That was only fitting, he thought, for one of six Heisman Trophy candidates invited on the nationwide tour; for a player who had *arrived*. Then he met the other five players: Ross Browner of Notre Dame, Terry Miller of Oklahoma State, Matt Cavanaugh of Pittsburgh, Ray Griffin of Ohio State, and Manu Tuiasosopo of UCLA. They all had new suits, too — one for every day of the tour.

Still, Nielsen had something they didn't have. And didn't want. A custom-made, removable cast.

The cast fit over his right hand and could be taken off when necessary, which was often as the ABC tour went from New York to Chicago to Atlanta to Dallas and, finally, to Los Angeles. It was one thing to have a broken right hand. It was another to advertise it in the media capitals of America. It wasn't going to help an aspiring Heisman winner's cause if he had a grip like a rock because it was a rock. In public, Gifford didn't wear the cast. The only problem then was avoiding shaking hands, which, by tour's end, he became quite good at.

He had broken his right hand on July 20 in a summer league softball game when he and a base runner rounding second base collided. When Nielsen asked Scovil if he could play softball in the summer, Scovil had said, "As long as you don't throw, sweat or slide." That was why he was playing second base. How could you get in trouble playing second base?

He called LaVell Edwards from the hospital.

"Coach, I gotta tell you something," he said, and then paused. "I broke my hand."

"No. Really?" said Edwards. "What's up?"

Nielsen had to wear the cast for four weeks. He did not practice in August two-a-days and had the cast removed only three days before the season opener, a rematch against the Kansas State team that had ruined Scovil's debut the year before. His right arm had atrophied and his hand was tender and had to be iced down before

48

the game. But by game time the old reflexes returned. Kansas State fell 39-0 as Nielsen completed twenty-seven of forty-five passes for two touchdowns and 318 yards.

He didn't practice the next week, and then threw six touchdown passes for 321 yards in a 65-6 win at Utah State that was broadcast regionally by ABC.

The craziness was happening all over again. For the first time in his twenty-six years at BYU, sports information director Dave Schulthess had a Heisman Trophy campaign to mount. Schulthess got a call from Paul Harvey, the syndicated radio newsman and champion of the flag, mom, and apple pie. Harvey had started a "Gifford Nielsen Watch" on his Monday morning show and wanted details from every Saturday's game. Like Lindberg flying the Pacific, the Gifford Nielsen story captured America's imagination. After BYU played New Mexico in game three, Harvey reported five touchdown passes and 273 yards in a 54-19 BYU rout. The Cougars were undefeated and had outscored their opponents 158-25. They were ranked thirteenth in the Associated Press poll and twelfth by UPI.

For the fourth game of the season, on the road against Oregon State in Corvallis, Oregon, Schulthess left a week early to stop at the media outlets in the Pacific Northwest and spread the word to all those who couldn't pick up Paul Harvey. *Sports Illustrated* flew a writer and photographer to Corvallis. They wanted Nielsen on their cover the following week.

Nielsen had already set thirteen school records and thirteen WAC records; and although he'd only started twenty-one games in his career, he was closing in on several NCAA career records. After just three games in 1977 he had thrown thirteen touchdown passes for nearly one thousand yards, and he hadn't thrown an interception. Scovil gave him the green light to do whatever he wanted. Sometimes the coach would merely raise his right arm on the sideline, which was their signal that it was Nielsen's play. Go ahead, surprise him.

Oregon State wasn't expected to present many problems. The Beavers had a tradition of not producing good football teams. In 1977 they were not a good football team. They were 1-3 coming into the BYU game and decided underdogs against the nationally ranked Cougars. When BYU took a 13-0 halftime lead after Nielsen threw two more touchdown passes, no one was surprised. He added another touchdown pass seventeen seconds into the second half for a 19-0 Cougar lead, and down on the field the *Sports Illustrated* photographer was looking for just the right shot for the cover.

Then the OSU defense started bringing a hard blitz. BYU countered by calling short pass plays to running backs Todd Christensen and Roger Gurley. Oregon State got the hint and went after Christensen and Gurley as though there was a bounty on them. They were often tackled before they got in position.

For one of the first times in its history, BYU was having to deal with a possessed underdog. The Beavers were mad. Finally members of the national media were in their press box, and there was more interest in an Oregon State football game than there had been in years. But all the hoopla had nothing to do with them. They were supposed to be the Washington Generals to the Harlem Globetrotters.

Well, not if they could help it. The atmosphere in the second half changed. Every tackle was with venom. The crowd suddenly got excited. It dawned on the Cougars that Oregon State wasn't on their side. They looked around to make sure they knew where they'd parked the bus. If they could just get out of Parker Stadium undefeated, and alive.

Oregon State answered BYU's early third-quarter touchdown with a drive and touchdown of its own. Moments later, under heavy pressure, Nielsen threw an interception. The pass wasn't off target, but it hit wide receiver John VanDerWouden in the chest and bounced into the hands of Oregon State linebacker Kent Howe, who returned the ball thirty-two yards for a touchdown. BYU's lead was quickly cut to 19-13. Then, as the fourth quarter began, Nielsen was intercepted again. OSU middle linebacker Gene Dales caught the pass in the flat and returned it seventy-nine yards for a touchdown.

The Cougars were getting that feeling you get when you know it's not your day. All their mistakes were being turned into touchdowns.

BYU got the ball back with seven minutes remaining, trailing 24-19. On second down on his own eight-yard line, Nielsen dropped back near the goal line. His intent was to strike quickly. Wide receiver Mike Chronister, the primary receiver, was running a post pattern. Nielsen's attention was all downfield. He didn't see left tackle Kelly Harris, his old Provo High buddy, blocking an Oregon State defender to his left. He didn't see the two linemen—all five hundred pounds of them—fall backward as he released the ball. He *did* hear his knee pop. It sounded as though a guitar string had snapped. Nielsen had never had a leg injury, but when he stood up he knew something was wrong.

One incomplete pass later the Cougars had to punt. On the sidelines Nielsen checked his knee. It felt rubbery, but he could still walk. He returned for the next offensive series, which started at the BYU nineteen-yard line. On a first-down blitz an OSU linebacker, smelling blood, hit the knee again at the same angle. Another pop. Nielsen went into the first stages of shock, but he didn't take himself out. He stayed for eleven more plays. He completed three passes and got the Cougars a first-and-goal at the ten-yard line. The best passing team in America had four cracks at the end zone.

But Nielsen's drops were reduced to one step backward. He wasn't taking false steps, he wasn't taking any steps at all. He could not plant on his left leg.

Four straight passes fell incomplete.

They were the last college passes Gifford Nielsen would ever throw.

He hobbled to the sidelines and said to Edwards, "If we get the ball back, I can't go in. I can't walk." After an Oregon State punt Marc Wilson went in at quarterback for a final series that didn't work.

The team flew directly to Salt Lake City and then drove to Provo. Edwards sat next to Nielsen, telling him it would be all right. But Dr. Robert Metcalfe, the Cougars' orthopedic surgeon, had already been alerted, and they weren't letting Nielsen eat. You can't eat if you're going to have surgery.

Metcalfe knew knees. He knew good ones and bad ones and

ones that could be salvaged long enough to win a Heisman Trophy. He had helped promote the advancement of arthroscopic surgery, a minisurgical procedure that could be used for examinations and to repair minor tears. After an arthroscopy an athlete could be back on the playing field within a matter of weeks. When Metcalfe, along with trainers Rod Kimball and Marv Roberson, BYU athletic director Glen Tuckett, and Edwards, met Nielsen in Provo, he was hoping they could get by with an arthroscope. He lifted Nielsen's left knee and let it drop and knew immediately that wouldn't be possible. The medial collateral ligament, the major connecting ligament on the inside of the knee, had detached from the bone.

"I don't know how to tell you this," he said to Nielsen, "but your college football career is over. We should operate immediately."

Nielsen asked for a priesthood blessing, was given the blessing by Edwards, and underwent surgery at 3:00 A.M. They saved the ligament by stapling it to the bone. He would play football again. But in the NFL, not in college. He was an accident that had already happened. On his left leg he had a full-length cast—and this one couldn't be removed in public.

When Nielsen came out of the anesthesia, over two hundred people came to his hospital room. He received flowers and phone calls—one of the first was from Virgil Carter, BYU's first All-American quarterback. Teammates called and dropped by. Some fans couldn't accept the reality of what had happened. They called Nielsen and asked why he didn't go to the headquarters of the Mormon church and get healed. Edwards got calls to the same effect.

Late in the afternoon, when no other visitors were there, Scovil came by. He had sunglasses on, and he didn't take them off.

Nielsen was in the hospital for a week and, for a person who one minute was chasing the Heisman Trophy and the next was being fit for a cast, he was remarkably upbeat. A model patient, the nurses called him.

The night he was released from the hospital Nielsen got a phone call that put his accident in better perspective. His brother-in-law, Elwin Atwood, a dentist in Price, Utah, had been in an accident that took his leg off just below the knee. "That really put into perspective what I was having to go through," said Nielsen.

When his brother-in-law came out of surgery the next day, Gifford called. He challenged him to a race on their crutches.

Two days later, up and down the corridor in the Price hospital, they raced.

Elwin won.

MARC WILSON

"GONNA FLY NOW"
— *Theme from* Rocky, 1977

*H*e geared down his 1974 Ford Pinto and pulled into the hospital parking lot. It had been nearly twenty-four hours since the game at Oregon State, when Gifford Nielsen couldn't walk and he had been sent in as the BYU quarterback for the last three plays. No one in the outside world knew what condition Nielsen's left knee was in, or whether he could still play football. This included his understudy, who was more than a little curious. Marc Wilson had finally taken this little drive to the Utah Valley Hospital to find out.

He was doing his best to remain positive. The fact that Nielsen was in the hospital was not a good sign for either of them, true; but maybe the doctors were just being careful. Maybe he was there for observation. Maybe they'd found he had tonsillitis.

Wilson walked down the hall to Nielsen's room. Visitors coming out were talking in hushed tones. Wilson soon found out why. When he walked in he saw that Nielsen was wearing a full-length cast on his left leg.

"Wanta sign it?" Nielsen asked.

On the drive back to his apartment at Wymount Terrace, where he lived in married-student housing with his wife, Colleen, Wilson pounded the steering wheel in his Pinto. "The team's all yours," Nielsen had told him. "I don't want the team," Wilson was now saying, over and over again.

He took a quick inventory of where he stood: He was taking over from an All-American quarterback who had won seventeen games in his past twenty-two starts and who had passed for enough yardage to land at the feet of the Heisman Trophy. And he was taking over for him with a game coming up Saturday at Colorado State against a team that was 5-0 and loaded with NFL-bound defensive players who were still not happy about the previous year's BYU game when they had been humiliated 42-18.

To get ready for BYU II, Bubba Baker and Mike Bell, the leaders of the CSU Rams' defense, had printed up and were wearing T-shirts that said "Gifford Nielsen Fan Club" on them. Nielsen had thrown four touchdown passes against them the year before, and they hadn't forgotten. This was their way of letting Nielsen know. If he was now going to get out of a rematch with a lame excuse, they'd have to take it out on his replacement.

Wilson knew he couldn't be ready in a week. He had thrown all of twenty passes in his major college career, and while he had completed eighteen of them, they had come at the end of games when the other team was also playing its reserves and their incentive was gone. He did not feel an integral part of the BYU offense. In their daily one-hour sessions, Nielsen and quarterback coach Doug Scovil had never invited him to listen in. From that he'd gathered that Scovil didn't like him. The coach only gave him occasional comments. When Wilson had complained about it to Nielsen, Gifford had brushed it off. "That's just Sco," he said. "When it's your turn, you'll know what you need to know."

Now it was his turn. And Sco was giving him a crash course in BYU quarterbacking.

Wilson wasn't eating, or sleeping, or going to class. He was hanging onto Doug Scovil like he was a lifeboat. When Scovil said "meet," Wilson asked when.

Scovil said two things that did cheer Wilson up slightly. He told him he knew he wasn't Gifford Nielsen and he wasn't going to make him play the way Gifford played; and he asked him, "Okay, what would you like to do?"

Taking the day off was not an option.

"Well," said Wilson, "I like to run."

They conceived a game plan. Scovil decided that, whereas Nielsen needed good pocket protection and did well in a pure drop-back system, Wilson was quicker and not as developed at staying in the pocket and picking teams to pieces before they could do vice versa. So they would change the offense to allow Wilson to leave the pocket and roll out and run if he wanted. BYU had rolled out on maybe four plays the entire season. This would be a new look. If all went well, it might create a new fan club.

That was on paper. In Marc Wilson's stomach something else was going on. He was not a walking, talking Dale Carnegie course. He found some stationery and wrote his parents. He told them he was dedicating the CSU game to them, the reason for doing the dedication now being that he might never play another game.

Before leaving for Colorado State the BYU team went by the hospital to see Nielsen. Wilson asked him one more time, "Are you sure you can't play?"

"You'll knock 'em dead," said Nielsen, who added, "and see if you can get me one of those shirts."

Out of sheer exhaustion, Wilson slept the night before the game. Prior to kickoff he huddled with Scovil one more time. Scovil had taken his dark glasses off after he'd left Nielsen's room in the hospital, and kept them off. Like life, football went on. He acted no more worried than if this was a practice scrimmage. That calmed Wilson down enough to get him to the starting line.

It might have gone badly with a slow start. But Wilson took the opening snap, dropped back, rolled to his right, and found himself as alone as the Golden Eagles in nearby Rocky Mountain National Park — and almost as protected. He completed a pass to Roger Gurley for nine yards. His next two passes were also complete. In six plays the Cougars scored, on a thirty-eight-yard Wilson-to-Tod Thompson touchdown pass.

He hadn't had time to freeze up.

It would be years before they got over this game in Ft. Collins, the day an unheralded, unheard-of soph-omore from BYU threw *seven* touchdown passes. BYU won 63-17. The victory was all the more remarkable in that Bubba Baker, Mike Bell, Mark Nichols, and Cliff Featherstone — each of them destined to be on the 1977 all-WAC defense team — never laid a hand on the new kid. They got to Marc Wilson in Ft. Collins as much as they'd gotten to Gifford Nielsen in Provo.

Wilson completed fifteen of twenty-five passes for 332 yards against the Rams. His seven touchdown passes set a conference record. He ran for an eighth touchdown. After the game Scovil said Wilson not only reminded him of Gifford Nielsen but also of Roger Staubach. "They both scramble, they both throw well on the run," he said.

Wilson returned to Provo an overnight sensation. He was named *Sports Illustrated*'s Player of the Week, the quarterback in UPI's national Backfield of the Week, and the AP Back of the Week. He responded with a rookie's nonchalance. This game was so easy they should outlaw him. To make it fair the defense should get thirteen men. For his next dedication . . .

The team traveled next to Laramie, Wyoming, where the University of Wyoming Cowboys came out of the film room bleary-eyed from watching rerun after rerun of "Marc Wilson Destroys CSU." The Cowboys vowed not to be similarly embarrassed. They weren't. BYU barely hung on for a 10-7 win as Wilson, the boy wonder, set his second WAC record in as many weeks. He was intercepted six times.

In just two weeks he had already ridden the roller coaster from top to bottom. As he was about to find out, that was just for starters.

SEATTLE, WASHINGTON
1957-1974

If you grew up in Seattle in the 1960s you were not alone.

Boeing was building airplanes, the Space Needle was shining all the way to Vancouver, and young families by the thousands were spilling out of the Seattle city limits up and down the Puget Sound. When Doug and Carroll Wilson bought a home in the Shoreline area of the northern suburb of Ridgecrest, their four children—Dru, Marc, Ronella and Shea—joined a cast of thousands.

Kids were everywhere. Everything was young. Greater Seattle was developing, not developed. The Seahawks of the NFL and the Mariners of major league baseball hadn't yet come to town. The SuperSonics of the NBA wouldn't arrive until 1967. There was no Kingdome. Games were for kids. If parents were smart, they didn't use day-care centers. They used Little Leagues.

In the Shoreline area a group of parents established the Univac Boy's Club and signed up boys by the station-wagon load. Univac had a motto that they never turned a kid away; they also had a motto that winning was more fun than losing. With their strength in numbers they responded accordingly. Some Univac kids never lost. One of them was Marc Wilson, whose Univac basketball team won one hundred straight games.

Marc became addicted to winning. In everything. When he was a seventh-grader he signed up to play the trombone with the junior high band. He had been playing the trombone casually for a couple of years in elementary school. They assigned him to the A band, which was prestigious in itself for a seventh-grader, and made him third chair on the trombone row, in back of two ninth-graders.

That night, as he was reading the paper, Doug Wilson heard unusual sounds coming from the basement. Marc was playing scales on his trombone. The next night he heard it again, the next night also.

"What's the big push," Marc's father finally asked.

"There are two ahead of me," said Marc.

By the eighth grade he was first chair. Then he quit.

But he didn't quit sports. He was raised playing football in the street, or baseball at one of the six diamonds at nearby Hamlin Park, where there was no lack of people to play with or against. From the Ridgecrest area alone dozens of kids would go on to play major college sports, and some would go on to play professionally. There was Ray Pinney, who went to the Pittsburgh Steelers; and Mike Mahoski and Kurt Fabrizio, who played professional baseball; and Mark McGrath, who went on to play with the Washington Redskins and then returned home to play for the Seahawks; and Mike O'Brien, who became a wide receiver for Cal-Berkeley.

The Seattle youth teams played anyone and anywhere. By the time he entered high school, Marc had already played in one sport or another in every state in the Northwest. He had gone to Alaska when he was sixteen as the youngest member of the Cheney Studs, a Seattle-area semipro baseball team.

All of this created logistical problems for Marc — such as when he was fourteen and trying to become both an Eagle Scout and the next Sandy Koufax. He signed up for Scout camp at Camp Parsons, fifty miles away in the mountains, and he also registered to play every day in the Little League baseball play-offs in Seattle.

He commuted between the two daily and never did become an Eagle Scout, or, for that matter, the next Sandy Koufax.

It wasn't easy being a full-time achiever.

Marc's parents helped. Doug Wilson, a supervisor for the Washington State Liquor Control Board, believed his children should participate in all the youth activities they could manage, and he discouraged them from working formal jobs. He held two jobs himself, and Carroll Wilson helped in the lunch room at Meridian Elementary School to help pay for tap dance lessons and football registrations.

Marc gave them no trouble. He kept his room as neat as an army barracks. He did his schoolwork. He was a busy, serious kid who didn't like to stop or even slow down. Once, when he was playing baseball in a Little League all-star tournament, he blocked a ground ball with his face. He was carried to a nearby drinking fountain where they washed the blood off. He looked like he'd been in a hockey brawl. But nothing appeared broken so he insisted on returning to the game. He didn't miss an inning, which was more than could be said for his two front teeth. They both died. He eventually got them capped, but not until ten years later.

Being intense had its downside. The other boys at church, for instance, didn't quite know what to make of Marc, who tended to be quiet and reserved. They'd choose him last when they played basketball in the church gym.

He was not a rah-rah type and did not have a lot of outside loyalties. The University of Washington campus was just twenty minutes away, but he didn't go to the Huskies' games or hang big block W's on his wall. But neither did he have boyhood leanings toward Brigham Young University. Prior to his senior season of high school, he wasn't aware there was a BYU.

Like hundreds of other colleges, BYU knew there was a Marc Wilson. Being 6'5" and close to two hundred pounds in high school tends to attract attention. Marc had always been bigger and taller than most of the other kids — including his brother, Dru, who was older by three years but six inches shorter and thirty pounds lighter. And Marc was naturally coordinated. Sports weren't a chore. He moved from one to the next with ease. He was all-city and all-state as a pitcher in baseball. He was all-city and all-state as a forward in basketball. And he was all-city as a quarterback and free safety in football.

Ironically, it was football that he almost left behind. After the last year of Little League, he thought he'd had enough of football and did not go out for the Shorecrest High School sophomore team. But midway through the season he relented. He didn't know what to do with all that free time. He went out for both free safety and quarterback to make up for lost time, and played both ways.

Ever since his second year of Little League football, when he was ten, Marc had been a quarterback. The coach of that team was faced with a group of would-be Terry Bradshaws. Marc was one of the few kids who didn't ask to be quarterback. He got the job because he could throw the ball farther than anyone on the team, and because it got the coach off the hook.

By his senior year in high school Marc had played quarterback long and well enough to have a steady stream of recruiters following him around. But then, in the third game of the season in 1974, his jaw was broken in a game between Shorecrest High and crosstown rival Lincoln High. Ironically, Marc's future wife, Colleen, was a cheerleader for Lincoln High. As they carried Marc off the field that day she was busy leading the Lincoln studentbody through a chorus of "Hit him again, hit him again, harder, harder."

Most of the college recruiters backed off as if the broken jaw were either an incurable or a communicable disease. The University of Washington gave Marc only token interest. But one school that didn't back off was BYU. LaVell Edwards and Dave Kragthorpe, Edwards' offensive coordinator, made themselves at home in the Wilson household, where they talked of the passing offense they were shaping in Provo and emphasized that they had just ridden the passing arm of Gary Sheide to the school's first-ever bowl game.

Marc was interested in listening to any basketball and baseball offers that came his way. Edwards told him he could play both baseball and football at BYU. That clinched the deal. Through the wires clamping his jaw shut he asked, "Where do I sign?"

1975-1976

He'd never been to Utah, but he was not without roots there. Marc Wilson's mother grew up in Harrisville, a small town north of Ogden. His grandfather had been the first sheriff of Ogden, and Marc was distantly related to Brigham Young.

Wilson pitched two games for the BYU junior varsity baseball team in the spring of 1976, his freshman year, but he got homesick and went back to Seattle. That was it for baseball. There was a new electricity around the BYU football program. A third-year sophomore named Gifford Nielsen had rallied the team to six wins in its last eight games of the 1975 season, and had passed with increasing success. And even though Wilson had a formidable challenger in fellow freshman quarterback Danny Hartwig, a rifle-armed recruit from Walnut Creek, California, he thought he might have a future in football. He settled in for the long haul. After trading off quarterbacking the freshman team with Hartwig in 1975, he agreed to a redshirt year the next fall.

The following summer he returned to Seattle and married Colleen, the cheerleader from Lincoln High. They had met at a church dance not long after he had broken his jaw.

In the fall of 1976 they moved into a one-bedroom apartment in the married-student-housing complex at Wymount Terrace in Provo. With the exception of moving across the hall to a two-bedroom unit two years later when they had their first child, Travis, they stayed settled. Marc enrolled to study economics, bought a used 1974 Ford Pinto, had his hair cut at the campus barbershop, reported to fall football practice as a redshirt, and got serious about academics and college life.

He was a prototype student-athlete, which, translated, means he went to class and knew where the library was. Even when football became more demanding, he never strayed from academics. A member of the National Honor Society in high school, with a 3.83 grade point average, Wilson kept it up at BYU, where he would graduate with a 3.6 grade point average in economics. He studied constantly. On road trips he always took his books. He was accepted for postgraduate work at both law school (BYU) and MBA school (at the prestigious St. Mary's College in San Francisco).

Socially, Wilson was also an atypical football player. He led the team in friends who *didn't* play football. This included any number of professors. His best friend became Paul Harman, a pre-law student he met in a religion class. His best friend on the football team became Brent Johnson, a walk-on wide receiver/ kicker from Salt Lake City.

He didn't just play the sports that were paying him scholar-ships. There was skiing in Provo, so he got hooked on that — so hooked that every President's Day for four years he and Harman went to Exhibition on Sun Valley's Bald Mountain in Idaho to pay their respects to the best bump run in the world. A football coach would have developed ulcers following Wilson around. He liked to ski jump and water ski as well, and when Harman, a rancher's son from Riverton, Utah, introduced him to rodeo, he gave that a try.

But he was no Indiana Jones. He didn't do any of it for fortune and glory.

He was certainly no media darling in waiting. He had no desire to be a public figure. Even after years of practice he could barely tolerate talking to the press. For one thing, he was shy; for another, he was extremely sensitive and defensive about anything written. There was a game later in his BYU football career in which he threw an interception and then tackled the defensive back re-turning the ball upfield. He was knocked momentarily unconscious and after the game couldn't remember anything that happened. "My most enjoyable game," he'd boast to friends, because he didn't have to talk to the press afterwards. He couldn't tell them anything.

But in the fall of 1976 the press was no problem. Wilson was a member of the world's most anonymous fraternity, the redshirt squad, and he watched and waited as Gifford Nielsen passed the Cougars to a 9-3 record and a berth in the Tangerine Bowl. When Wilson beat out Hartwig for the number-two quarterback spot in the 1977 spring drills, he was just one step away from being first chair, and that was good, because he was going to be a sophomore that season, and Nielsen was heading into his final year, and you can't have it set up much better than that.

1977

Marc Wilson's standards turned out to be no different than Gifford Nielsen's.

After his auspicious seven-touchdown start against Colorado State, and his inauspicious six-interception follow-up against Wyoming, he got down to the business of meeting daily with Scovil and learning how to steer the passing machine he had suddenly and unexpectedly inherited. Like Nielsen, he was a quick learner.

In his third start, against the University of Arizona, he worked the stage in Provo for the first time and threw twenty-three completions in forty-three attempts for 334 yards and two more touchdowns in a 34-14 win. All this in front of a sellout homecoming crowd in Cougar Stadium.

If that didn't clinch his hometown popularity, the next week, when the University of Utah came to Provo, left no doubt.

In that game, a 38-8 BYU win, Wilson had been taken out early in the fourth quarter after already throwing for 555 yards and four touchdowns. Then someone in the press box discovered Wilson was within six yards of the NCAA record for most yards passing in a game. The news was wired down to the field. In the fourth quarter Scovil sent Wilson back in the game. "Throw any pattern you want to," he said.

Seeing the Cougars' first-string quarterback reentering the game with his team down by three touchdowns and time about to expire did nothing for Utah coach Wayne Howard's disposition. He threw his clipboard to the ground as Wilson threw a sideline pattern to wide receiver John VanDerWouden that was good for eight yards and the record. He threw his coaching headset down seconds later when Wilson threw another pass, again for eight yards to VanDerWouden, this time for another BYU touchdown.

For his part, Scovil was never bashful about scoring touchdowns. Often when the game was out of reach and Edwards would call for running plays to eat up the clock, Scovil would call for passing plays anyway. In his offensive team meetings on Friday nights he would talk about "lighting up the scoreboard so it looks like something out of Las Vegas — numbers spinning, lights flashing."

"It was never a question of winning with Doug Scovil, it was a question of how many we were going to score," said Wilson. "He was a great teacher, a great motivator, and, more than anything else, a great game coach. He knew what the defenses were going to do. He just knew. He'd get that grin on his face, and 95 percent of the time he'd be right. He made it all go."

In all, the Cougars went 6-1 in 1977 with Wilson at quarterback, losing only to Arizona State on the road. They tied for the WAC title and Wilson set four NCAA records. Three came in a 30-27 win over Long Beach State, for most yards gained in a half (339), most passing yards gained in a half (326), and most passes completed in a half (twenty-seven). The fourth record was the single-game passing yardage record of 571 set against Utah. For the abbreviated season Wilson had twenty-four touchdown passes while completing 164 of 277 passes for 2,418 yards.

As an encore to the 1977 season the Cougars accepted an invitation from the Japanese government to play against two Japanese all-star teams. They spent ten days in the Orient, learned how to use chopsticks, visited shrines, ate sushi, and beat the seriously out-manned (read, outweighed) Japanese in the two games by more than a combined one hundred points. Wilson played only sparingly. The Japanese were impressed by the Cougars and invited them back the next year but told them to bring their own opposition. (BYU accepted and brought Nevada-Las Vegas.)

As he rode the bullet train from Nagoya to Tokyo to begin the long trip home to Seattle for Christmas Eve, Wilson reflected on the past two-and-a-half months and how quickly it had all come together. The only complaint he'd heard was from the Utah coach, for running up the score, and in Provo that made you a candidate for knighthood.

In Tokyo, Jim McMahon, the team's punter and a reserve quarterback, had bought a T-shirt that said "No. 1" in Japanese, and had worn it constantly. Wilson hadn't taken it as a warning, but he should have.

1978

Two things happened as the 1978 season dawned that had a direct impact on Marc Wilson: Doug Scovil accepted an offer from the Chicago Bears to coach their receivers, and Jim McMahon ran out of patience.

As a freshman the year before, McMahon had been the Cougars' number-one punter and number-four quarterback, and had spent the season wondering why.

A brash, cocky and talented recruit from Roy, Utah, McMahon did not believe in seniority. He saw no reason he shouldn't be starting for BYU ahead of anyone, including Marc Wilson, who threw seven touchdown passes in his first college game. McMahon was as outwardly competitive as Wilson was inwardly competitive. In spring practice their battle began in earnest — a battle that would be Wilson's toughest challenge at BYU. Winning the WAC was easy compared to this. Historical perspective would help later on: Here were two NFL-qualified quarterbacks thrown together, through no fault of their own, on the same bench in the same season. Each had a type-A, achieve-or-else personality. Each was talented. Each hated to lose. Something had to give.

Wilson's cause was not helped at all when Scovil left for Chicago. The new quarterback coach was a strong-minded drill sergeant type named Wally English who had been an assistant coach at Kentucky, Arkansas, Virginia Tech, and Nebraska, and most recently had been on the staff of the Detroit Lions. English, who backed up Johnny Unitas as a college quarterback at Louisville, sized up the BYU situation quickly and determined that he would not be Doug Scovil's replacement. He would be his own genius. He brought a variety of new formations to the offense with plays patterned after the motion game that was working well for the Dallas Cowboys. Despite using the same playbook, he changed virtually everything that had worked under Scovil. Wally English was not devoid of ego.

Neither was he enamored with Wilson.

If you wanted a rah-rah type in the huddle, a quarterback who barked orders and ripped off his chin strap when a receiver missed a pass, Marc Wilson was not your guy. Wally English wanted that kind of quarterback. In the locker room one afternoon not long after practice had started in August, English walked up to Wilson and told him he'd never make it in the pros, that he was too quiet and too nice.

Wilson told him that if he had to make it by being a jerk, then he didn't want to make it.

As coach-player relationships go, this one was rapidly developing along the lines of Billy Martin-Reggie Jackson.

Now McMahon, he *did* bark orders in the huddle, and he had been known on occasion to stare down receivers who had run a down-and-in when they were supposed to run a down-and-out. English liked that. He also liked the fact that McMahon had not been Doug Scovil's quarterback.

Throw into this whole scenario the fact that McMahon and Wilson, as white Anglo-Saxon males, were as opposite as, say, Pat Boone and Mick Jagger, and a real soap opera was developing.

By the fall, English moved McMahon into an alternating practice situation with Wilson. They took turns running the first-team offense, even though Wilson, after a 6-1 starting record the year before, was officially first string.

Underwhelmed by all this confidence, Wilson—who responded as defensively to coaching criticism as he responded to criticism in the media—started the opening game against Oregon State and produced a fifteen of thirty-eight performance for just 193 passing yards. The Cougars barely hung on for a 10-6 win in a game that wasn't offensive to anyone. The next week Wilson started and lost 24-16 to Arizona State. In the third game, a 32-6 win over Colorado State, he came out early with a hamstring injury and McMahon took advantage of his opportunity by completing seven of nine passes for 112 yards and a touchdown. Still, Wilson had his backers—most notably Edwards, who liked to change starters as often as Switzerland liked to go to war. So Wilson started the fourth game, at New Mexico, and went the distance for a 27-23 win. Then he started the fifth and sixth games, against Utah State and Oregon, but was replaced in both by McMahon. When McMahon took over in Oregon on the downside of a 16-3 score and passed the Cougars to a 17-16 win, Wilson was out of a full-time job.

With his keen sixth sense and his ability to scramble out of all the new motion that was going on, McMahon put some life into English's complicated offensive patterns and held on as the starter until the eleventh game of the season, at Hawaii, when a knee injury forced him to sit that game out. McMahon had beaten UTEP, Wyoming, and San Diego State; but in his fourth start, in the tenth game of the season, he had been made to pay for Wilson's transgression. The game was the annual rematch with the University of Utah. The Utes hadn't beaten BYU in the Edwards era, which was six years old, and they came out meekly and spotted McMahon and the Cougars a 16-0 halftime lead. Then, thinking about what had happened the year before in Provo when Wilson poured it on and set his NCAA single-game, passing-yardage record, they fired up and rallied for a 23-22 win. To add injury to insult, in the fourth quarter McMahon pivoted too quickly and severely hyperextended his knee.

At Hawaii, against a good 6-3 Rainbow team, Wilson — without having to worry about McMahon — completed twenty-one passes in thirty attempts for 291 yards and two touchdowns. He had come back to life. And against Nevada-Las Vegas in Japan he won again, with three touchdown passes in a 28-24 win that was easier than it sounded.

But the starting job was still McMahon's, who had an excuse from the doctor. Or so it seemed at the time.

As the WAC champion Cougars took their tumultuous 9-3 record to San Diego for the first-ever Holiday Bowl, to be played December 22, 1978, in San Diego Stadium against a Navy team they were supposed to defeat by two touchdowns, a microcosm of the 1978 season was about to unfold.

In the weeks before the game the quarterback controversy heated up again. At the practice sessions in San Diego, Wilson and McMahon took turns running the offense. Then Edwards, in

68

a surprise move—those most surprised were McMahon and English—named Wilson as BYU's Holiday Bowl starter.

In the opening quarter against Navy, every play English called was a motion play—the kind more suited to McMahon. By the second quarter, with the score tied 3-3, Wilson was out and McMahon was in. He put the Cougars ahead at the half, 9-3, with a touchdown pass to Mike Chronister, and he scored himself on a two-yard plunge for a 16-3 lead in the third quarter.

But before long BYU's lack of consistent offense started to tell. Led by wide receiver Phil McConkey, Navy caught and passed the fading Cougars in the second half and won 23-16 on the strength of thirteen unanswered points in the last fifteen minutes. Wilson got a second appearance midway through the fourth quarter, but he was sacked on first down for a loss of twelve yards, and then threw two passes that were both incomplete.

Between the two of them, Wilson and McMahon connected on sixteen of thirty-four passes for 181 yards and were intercepted twice. Wilson was seven of sixteen for forty-eight yards with an interception, and McMahon was nine of eighteen for 133 yards with an interception. It was an uncharacteristic end to an uncharacteristic year. After spending the latter half of the 1976 season and the entire 1977 season ranked in the top twenty, and after leading the nation in passing both those seasons, BYU dropped to eighth in passing and spent the entire season without being ranked. And at 9-4 the Cougars had their worst season in three years.

The season had taken a heavy emotional toll on Wilson. He was worn out. He had no problem personally with McMahon. But he had a big problem with not knowing where he stood, and with playing for a coach who didn't want him. He was talking to himself. It kept him up nights. It affected his home life. The strain was so obvious that BYU President Dallin Oaks called Wilson to console him.

After the Holiday Bowl he carried his problem home with him to Seattle, where he had time to think and where he came to a conclusion. When he got back to campus in January to start the winter semester, he went into LaVell Edwards' office and told him he was quitting football.

It was like John Wayne giving up Westerns, like Liberace giving up the piano. When you've played the game your whole life, and you got your jaw broken, and you were a national Back of the Week, it isn't easy to walk away from football while you still have eligibility left. But enough was enough, and Marc Wilson had had enough.

He told Edwards he was going to go to law school and wanted to concentrate on his studies.

Edwards let it go. He knew something Wilson didn't know. Something that might change his mind. He knew that Wally English had just accepted a coaching offer from the University of Pittsburgh. And if anyone thought it would be impossible to ever again get a Doug Scovil at BYU they were wrong.

Scovil was coming back.

The quarterback coach hadn't had such a pleasant year, either. The Bears had gone 7-9 and finished fourth out of five in the NFC's Central Division. Worse than that, the Bears rarely threw the football. Scovil kept in touch with Edwards, and when they were talking on the phone one day not long after the Holiday Bowl Edwards had asked him, "Would you be interested in coming back?"

"I would," said Scovil, "if we don't have to look like the Dallas Cowboys."

Not long after Wilson announced his intended retirement, Edwards summoned the football team together for a short meeting in the fieldhouse. "I'd like to introduce you to someone most of you already know," he said, after which he asked his old/new offensive coordinator, Doug Scovil, to say a few words.

"Men, I don't know what happened while I was gone," Scovil said. "But I want you to know I spent a year in Chicago, in the National Football League, and right here we have a quarterback better than anybody we had there."

He pointed directly at Marc Wilson.

Sitting in his chair, Wilson called out a silent audible as he sensed a new beginning. He wouldn't be retiring his arm just yet after all.

1979

Nowhere do they treat football like they treat football in Texas, so there was no rational reason for Marc Wilson to be in anything even close to a good mood as the BYU punting unit passed him on its way to midfield.

It was the fourth quarter of the opening game of the 1979 season, BYU was trailing the Texas A&M Aggies 17-10, and the Aggies had the ball and the wild support of forty thousand A&M fans.

Due to construction at Kyle Field on the Texas A&M campus in College Station, the game was being played at Rice Stadium in Houston. But that only made everything louder. The Texas fans had a forty-five-minute drive to get in the mood, and there was plenty for them to get in the mood for. The Aggies had Curtis Dickey, the running back voted most likely to succeed that year in the Southwest Conference, and they had enough surrounding him to gain mention in virtually every preseason top twenty list, including the AP and UPI polls, which had them rated eighteenth.

For BYU there was this: At no time in its history had one of its football teams ever beaten a team outside the conference ranked in the top twenty.

Now, for some reason, behind by a touchdown in the final quarter, Wilson was having premonitions that the whammy was about to end.

Of course, it could have been the fever talking.

Less than twenty-four hours earlier Wilson had tried to throw passes while practicing in an empty Rice Stadium, and he had to have someone help him to the bench. He had a temperature of 103 degrees. The first thing the team doctor did, before sending him back to his hotel room, was check for gangrene. Doctors worry about gangrene when stitches from an appendectomy have recently been removed.

Other football players have knee injuries, or shoulder separations, or broken noses, or fingers that go out of joint. Before their senior seasons, Gary Sheide had injured his shoulder and Gifford Nielsen had broken his hand — each while playing softball. Before his senior season, Wilson had come up with a new twist. He ruptured his appendix.

For a long time he didn't know it was ruptured. He had been on a pack trip with Neils Tidwell, a teammate and friend, in the Sawtooth Mountains in Idaho when the appendicitis attack occurred. They were twenty-five miles in the back country at the time and Wilson passed the pain off as a bad stomachache, probably from some wild berries he had eaten. It hurt, but it wasn't anything worse than what linebackers did to him when they had him down. He wanted to keep fishing. Tidwell had promised him they were going to knock 'em dead, and in two days Wilson hadn't had so much as a nibble. But when the pain got so bad that he couldn't sit on his horse, he said maybe they'd better pack him out of there. Wilson propped himself against the saddlehorn as Tidwell and his brother, David, took turns riding behind him, holding him up. They got him into Nampa, Idaho, that way, where they put him on the next train to Provo.

Back in Provo, Wilson contacted the team doctor, who told him he had the flu and gave him some pills. He started to feel a little better, well enough for a round of golf. It appeared he was totally out of the woods because soon thereafter he passed the team physical.

But then the pain got bad again, so bad that Wilson couldn't get from his bed to the telephone. He reached the cord and pulled the phone off the hook and called the team doctor, telling him that maybe he had passed the team physical but there was still something definitely wrong.

They rushed him to the hospital and discovered the rupture, by now eight days old, and performed the appendectomy.

The worst part was that the Tidwells went back into the Sawtooths after dropping Wilson off in Nampa — and did knock them dead. Or so they said.

Wilson hadn't had to go through August two-a-days. There

was that consolation. But he couldn't play golf, either. Or eat. His weight dropped to 179 pounds—not bad if you're a 5'10" cornerback, but definitely on the anorexic side for a 6'5" quarterback. Wilson would have been content to let his actual weight remain a mystery, but a pro scout—and there was more than one lurking around prior to his senior year—asked if he'd get on the scales. There wasn't much he could do, and soon it was all over campus. He was down to 179.

The mending process went slowly. By the first weekend in September, Wilson flew with the team to Houston for the A&M game. He had only a few limited practice sessions to his credit and looked like one of the boat people that at the time were flooding into Houston from Cambodia. Even at that, the doctors were less worried about his emaciated condition than they were about infection.

The Cougars brought along Jim McMahon just in case. McMahon had logged some hospital time in the off-season himself. He'd had knee surgery and the plan, as conceived by Doug Scovil and LaVell Edwards, was to redshirt him in favor of the senior Wilson to ensure quarterback continuity for the Cougars for the next three seasons and to eliminate any controversy over which one should start. But now that plan was in trouble because the 1979 football season was about to begin and Marc Wilson was in his hotel room in Houston with a temperature of 103 degrees.

But if there's one thing fevers let you do, it's sleep. And there's another thing about fevers: When they leave, they leave all at once. Sometime between the time he went to sleep Friday night and woke up Saturday morning the fever left. He went to the coffee shop for breakfast and told Edwards he had defied physical science and that all 179 pounds of him would be available for duty in that night's game.

The news of Wilson's condition—the recent appendectomy, not the fever—had not escaped the attention of the Texas A&M football players, who did their best during pregame warmups to make the most of the situation. They ran past Wilson and rubbed their sides and groaned. They told him they'd see that he got back

73

to the hospital — quickly. When the game started they aimed for his appendix, wherever that was, as if it had a bull's-eye on it.

When Wilson threw five straight incompletions to start the game, the Aggies grew more confident. On the sidelines McMahon shifted from one foot to the other, ready to take off his red shirt.

But sometimes a quarterback gets a sense that he can move the ball, even if he hasn't already. Wilson had that sense. "There was never any panic," he said, "even though we had a hard time getting the lead."

The Aggies led at the half, 7-3, and the thinking was that the Cougars, Wilson especially, would get weaker as the game wore on in the hot and humid Texas night air. But Wilson and the Cougars got stronger. He completed four straight passes late in the third quarter for BYU's first touchdown, a twenty-yard pass to Dan Plater. The score was 14-10, Texas A&M leading. Then, after an A&M field goal had extended the Aggies' lead to 17-10 late in the fourth quarter, the Cougars blocked an A&M punt nineteen yards from the end zone. They scored in five plays on a three-yard pass from Wilson to Clay Brown.

There were fifty-two seconds left to play and BYU trailed by a point, 17-16. The Cougars were unranked, the Texas A&M Aggies were ranked and playing on their home field. BYU had nothing to lose. Edwards elected to go for the two-point conversion and a win rather than settle for a one-point kick and a probable tie. Time-out was called. Wilson went to the sideline for a conference with Scovil.

Wilson wanted to call a play titled "roll drop 43 pass," and he told Scovil why. The play called for a fake draw with a rollout to the left and a pass to either the fullback coming out of the backfield or to the wide receiver. A&M was in a four-man defensive front with man coverage on the receivers. That meant the middle linebacker would have to cover the halfback if he came hard at him out of the backfield, faking a draw, leaving the fullback, coming up underneath, free to get open. The only danger was if the weak-side linebacker didn't buy any of it and stayed man-to-man on the fullback.

"Risk we'll have to take," said Wilson.

74

"Let's try it," said Scovil.

The weak-side linebacker did buy it, and the play opened up like the field was a chalkboard. Fullback Mike Lacey ran the three yards into the end zone and turned around, waiting wide-eyed for the football. Bothered at the last instant by the Texas A&M defensive end, who was in his line of vision, Wilson released a pass that was low and hard and to Lacey's right. "It's not going to work," thought Wilson, "it's a terrible pass." But Lacey dove to his right and made a highlight-film catch. In an instant Rice Stadium went quieter than Gilley's Bar on a Sunday morning.

After fifty-eight years playing collegiate football, BYU had beaten a team ranked in the top twenty. In the locker room the moment was appropriately celebrated, although Wilson wasn't particularly flamboyant. He was relieved more than anything else. Now he could go back to bed.

He had thrown for only 165 yards against A&M, a total that would rank as his second lowest in three years as a BYU starter. But the stitches had held, and the Aggies had fallen, and the pollsters had been impressed. After taking a full season away from the top twenty, the Cougars were again ranked, at number twenty.

As Wilson and Scovil reunited for their encore season in 1979, scars remained from the year previous. McMahon, not Wilson, had been named the all-WAC quarterback in 1978. Despite his rush onto the collegiate scene as a sophomore as Nielsen's replacement, Wilson was nowhere to be found on lists of Heisman Trophy contenders. He believed the media had never gotten the situation right the year before, when he was criticized for the first time in his public life. He wanted no more of the press. He vowed not to open a newspaper the entire 1979 season. In what interviews he gave, begrudgingly, he talked of his ambition to be a lawyer. At home, football was rarely mentioned. He was determined to keep things in a new perspective. He knew how fast it could come and go.

He was the same quarterback. He hadn't changed. At practices he still didn't bark orders or lead cheers. On a team that had more than its share of experience, and leaders, it was the right touch. The 1979 BYU team would wind up with no less than thirteen all-conference players, including four members of Wilson's offensive line—Nick Eyre, Danny Hansen, Scott Nielson and Tom Bell—and his three favorite receivers—tight end Clay Brown, wide receiver Lloyd Jones, and running back Homer Jones.

Linebackers Glen Redd and Gary Kama, defensive backs John Neal and Bill Schoepflin, and lineman Glen Titensor were all-WAC and anchored a defense that would give up over twenty points only once in the entire regular season and would end the season as the twelfth best in the nation in scoring defense.

Marc Wilson didn't need to lead this band.

Tranquility set back in.

After the A&M win the Cougars beat Weber State and UTEP and Hawaii, all in Provo and all by comfortable margins.

A potential showdown loomed in the season's fifth game. BYU traveled to Utah State, where the Aggies awaited the 4-0 Cougars with a 3-1-1 team led by quarterback Eric Hipple. BYU was first in the country in passing; USU was second. Wilson was first in the country in total offense and passing; Hipple was second in both categories. A record crowd of 28,094—which broke the stadium record by 6,500—turned out in Utah State's Romney Stadium to see the contest. *Sports Illustrated* dispatched a writer for the potential drama. There was none. The Cougars won 48-24, with Wilson outdueling Hipple 372 yards to 182. BYU's Eric Lane scored a school record five touchdowns. When that week's *Sports Illustrated* hit the newsstands, the country learned all the details of Wilson's appendicitis in the Sawtooth Mountains and about everything that had happened since. In the history of college football no quarterback had ever thrown for more than seven, three-hundred-yard games in his career. Wilson's Utah State game gave him nine, and the season wasn't half over.

After every game Wilson called his father in Seattle and said the same thing: "This is getting crazy."

It got crazier at Wyoming, where Wilson threw four touchdowns and no interceptions to make amends for his six-interception nightmare of 1977. BYU won 54-14.

After beating Colorado State 30-7 (358 yards, three touchdown passes), BYU sent Wilson to the East Coast for media appearances. He traced the steps Gifford Nielsen had taken as an emerging Heisman Trophy candidate just two years earlier. The *New York Times* ran a lengthy feature story headlined, "B. Y. U.'s Wilson No Passing Fancy." Almost simultaneously the *Los Angeles Times* ran a story headlined, "Marc Wilson: No. 1 in the NFL Draft?" Professional scouting services were projecting him as a cinch high first-round NFL draftee, and potentially the first player taken.

By the time Utah fell 27-0—marking the first time in fifty-one years the Utes had failed to score a point against BYU— Wilson had thrown for over three hundred yards in nine straight games, and in those games the Cougars had outscored the opposition 366 to 94.

Going into the season's final regular season game the Cougars were 10-0 and had climbed to number nine in the national polls. Wilson had emerged as the premier quarterback in the country, and ABC television had decided it had gone long enough not putting this passing star on nationwide television.

For just the third time in its history, BYU football would be on a national television broadcast—not a regional broadcast, intended only for the Rocky Mountains, but a full-scale, second-game-of-the-Saturday-doubleheader broadcast. If they turned on their TV sets in Bangor, Maine, or Abilene, Texas, they'd see Marc Wilson and the Cougars.

For added intrigue, the Cougars' opponent, San Diego State, was having no slouch season, either. In just their second year in the WAC, the Aztecs were challenging for the title. They were 8-2 overall and 5-1 in the WAC, compared to BYU's 10-0 and 6-0. A win would give San Diego State a tie for the WAC championship and an automatic berth in the Holiday Bowl. The Aztec coach was Claude Gilbert, who in the past had brought along such prolific passers as Dan Fouts, Craig Penrose, and Jesse Freitas. Now he had two good young quarterbacks in Chris Schaefer and Mark Halda. What's more, for this game he had the home-field advantage. The game would be played in San Diego.

The weight of it all—the Heisman Trophy race, the national TV exposure, the nine straight three-hundred-yard games, the hype — got to Wilson in the pregame warmups. He could not throw a spiral.

Scovil stood behind Wilson as he threw the ball. He didn't change expression. The year had been a triumphant return for Scovil. Wally English, for all his determination the year before to not use Scovil's offense, had unwittingly made Scovil look all the better. After his year's sabbatical in the NFL, Scovil had brought the Cougars back to the same offense that had been in place when he left. And it had never looked more potent. As Scovil watched Wilson's wobbly nerve-wracked throws, he waited until he finally threw one that went almost straight.

"Great," he said, "that's enough."

Then ABC turned on its TV cameras and waited until the soap commercial was over and told BYU to go ahead and kick off. The Cougars held San Diego State on its first possession and forced a punt.

Two plays later Wilson threw a twenty-five-yard touchdown pass to Plater.

San Diego State was playing without a free safety, who was instead tied into the BYU halfback. He went wherever the halfback went. The Aztec defensive game plan centered on a ferocious rush. The idea was to stop the pass before it started. It was an all-or-nothing gamble.

On BYU's second series, after three plays, Wilson threw a forty-two-yard touchdown pass to Bill Davis.

On BYU's third series, he threw another touchdown pass, this one for fifty-seven yards to Eric Lane after two plays.

The game was five minutes old and all around the country viewers were already changing channels.

San Diego State stuck with its game plan, and BYU went on to win 63-14. Wilson played just over a half, completing thirteen of twenty-one passes for 278 yards.

Among those to shut off the television set long before the final score was posted was Lee Corso, the head football coach at Indiana University and, as his Hoosiers would be playing the game's winner in the Holiday Bowl, a particularly interested spectator.

As reported in the *Los Angeles Times*, Corso was in a hotel room in New York City with his close friend Dick Howser, then the manager of the New York Yankees. Corso and Howser settled in front of the TV as Corso positioned a notebook and pencil on the table in front of him.

"How good are these guys?" Howser asked.

"Pretty good," said Corso, "but we'll see."

Boom. Wilson throws his first touchdown.

"They look pretty good," said Howser.

Boom. Wilson throws his second touchdown.

"They *are* good," said Howser.

"You're right," said Corso.

Boom. Wilson throws his third touchdown.

"It's time to go to the bar," said Howser.

"Great idea," said Corso.

HOLIDAY BOWL II

The next time Lee Corso saw Marc Wilson he was not as complimentary.

The Indiana Hoosiers found their way to San Diego, where they were hardly the toast of the town. "Whoosiers?" the newspapers called them. An unranked 7-4 team, they were going to only the second bowl game in Indiana history (the other was the 1968 Rose Bowl, where the Hoosiers lost 14-3). They were installed as six-point underdogs and dropped to eight-point underdogs by game time. Ninth-ranked BYU was the NCAA total offense and passing yardage champion and had an eleven-game winning streak.

Wilson didn't miss a pass as BYU scored on its opening seventy-six-yard drive. On the Indiana sideline, Corso lost his composure, grabbed one of his defensive tackles when the ball was on the hashmark near the Indiana bench, and growled, "You see that guy," pointing at Wilson. "You go kill him."

BYU center Scott Nielson was about to hike the ball. But he saw what Corso did, and he started to laugh and couldn't stop. Then Wilson started to laugh, too. Nielson stood up. He couldn't hike the ball. The Cougars had to call time-out.

But as would be a BYU pattern in all its bowl games—brought on, perhaps, by cold weather in Provo and little work on the passing game in the month between the regular season and the bowl season—the offense sputtered. Though Wilson had only thrown seven interceptions in the last seven games of the regular season, he threw three against Indiana—mistakes that offset an otherwise business-as-usual, 380-yard night with twenty-eight completions on forty-three attempts and two touchdowns.

With 8:07 left to play, Indiana's Tim Wilber took in a BYU punt deflected by a BYU player and ran untouched for a sixty-two-yard touchdown.

The Indiana "Whoosiers?" had a 38-37 lead.

At 2:06 BYU started its final drive on its own twenty-one-yard line. In ten plays Wilson led the Cougars sixty-three yards down field. In the end zone sixteen yards away stood a 12-0 season and a certain top-ten final ranking. A Wilson run for six yards got the ball to the ten-yard line. Eleven seconds were left now. Wilson left the field. He had called his last play on the BYU roller coaster. It would be up to kicker Brent Johnson, Wilson's best friend on the team, to wrap this one up. Johnson had already kicked field goals of forty-six, twenty-nine, and twenty-eight yards, and had made four PATs. But he was not practiced at pressure kicks, not after an undefeated season that had never called for any. In the only game of the season settled by less than two touchdowns—the opener against Texas A&M—the clutch point-after attempt had been the two-point passing conversion.

Now Johnson stood looking at a twenty-seven-yard attempt. Little more than an extra point, really, although the ball was lined up on the right hashmark and the weight of the game, the season, and a first-ever BYU bowl win were hanging in the balance.

The time-out Indiana called didn't help matters.

Johnson hit the ball perfectly, but that was the end of it. He did not follow through. The ball was punched to the left. It looked like something Fernando Valenzuela might pitch. It never had a chance. On the Indiana sidelines there was great joy. The Cougars stayed on the field only long enough to accept the second-place trophy. Wilson stayed long enough to pick up his award as the Most Outstanding Offensive Player.

In the locker room the media crowded around Johnson's stall. When Wilson came in he immediately walked over to the reporters. What he did next wouldn't have surprised Wally English.

"I'd say my interceptions were what really killed us," he said.

It was a busy postseason. Marc Wilson was named the first team All-American quarterback on each of the five major teams — UPI, AP, Walter Camp, Football Coaches, and Football Writers. While throwing for 3,720 yards and twenty-nine touchdown passes, he set eighteen total offense and passing records. He also set nineteen WAC records. In the Heisman Trophy voting he finished third, behind Southern Cal's Charles White and Oklahoma's Billy Sims, two senior running backs who had been considered the top candidates since early in their junior seasons.

The touchdown clubs in Miami and Seattle each named him Player of the Year, the NCAA awarded him a postgraduate scholarship for his 3.6 grade point average in economics, and he was invited to play in both the Senior Bowl in Mobile, Alabama, and the East-West Shrine Game in San Francisco. He was on the winning side on both occasions; and after throwing three touchdowns in a 57-13 win in the Senior Bowl, he was presented a new Pontiac Firebird as the game's Most Valuable Player.

A driver was hired to transport the car from Mobile to Provo, so the first thing Wilson did after flying home was drive his yellow Pinto to the middle of the Wymount Terrace parking lot and hang a "Steal Me" sign in the window. When there were no takers, he gave the car to his geology professor, Jim Baer. Meanwhile, on the freeway off-ramp coming into Provo, the Firebird was in an accident. A tow truck hauled it to a garage for repairs. The episode capsulized Marc Wilson's five years as a Cougar. As with the seven touchdown passes at Colorado State followed by six interceptions at Wyoming; as with the all-WAC start as a sophomore followed by the tumultuous junior season in 1978; as with the undefeated season as a senior followed by a bowl win that seemed a cinch and then wasn't; the new car first represented the easy life, and then there it was, in the shop.

But as he got around campus mooching rides, and as his first-round selection by the Oakland Raiders would verify in that spring's NFL draft, neither Marc Wilson nor anyone else could help but marvel at the 1979 season—arguably the best and most prolific a college quarterback had ever had. An act that would be impossible to follow.

Or so it seemed at the time.

GARY SHEIDE

Greg and Gary, growing up

With Gary, baseball came first.

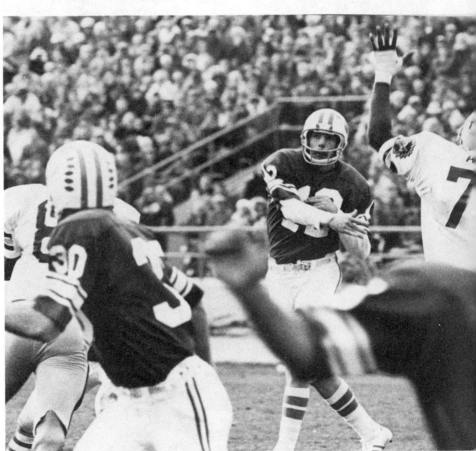

Passing by the Sun Devils in Cougar Stadium in 1974

His right arm didn't always cooperate.

BYU press book photo, 1974

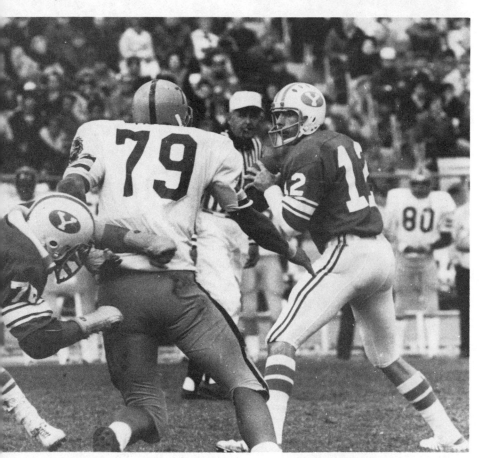

Gary striking a Namath-esque pose, 1973

GIFFORD NIELSEN

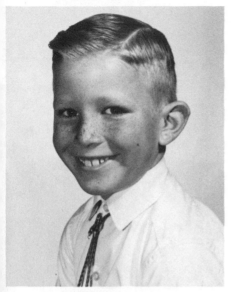

Young Giff is all smiles in the first grade.

Playing with an odd-shaped ball, 1974

Going to the ground against Wyoming

Wearing his designer cast in the 1977 preseason

BYU press book photo, 1976

Quarterbacking the Houston Oilers

MARC WILSON

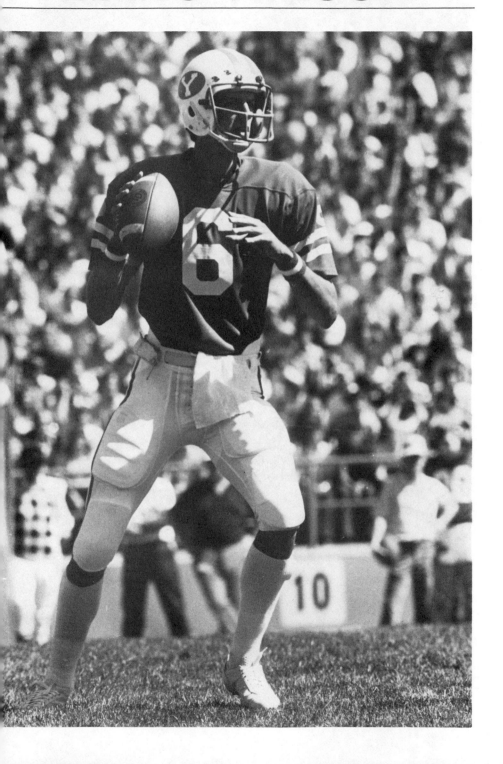

In full gear at age nine

Marc, age fourteen

Setting a controversial record against the Utes, 1977

Everything's in sync.

BYU press book photo, 1979

Quarterbacking the Los Angeles Raiders

JIM MCMAHON

Already a quarterback at age eleven

Striking a Heisman pose in 1981

Checking the options downfield

Celebrating the Miracle Bowl win, 1980

BYU press book photo, 1980

Quarterbacking the Chicago Bears, 1987

STEVE YOUNG

A fourth-grader in Connecticut

Grit and Steve

Beating Missouri and winning the Holiday Bowl, 1983

Looking to pass . . . or run

BYU press book photo, 1983

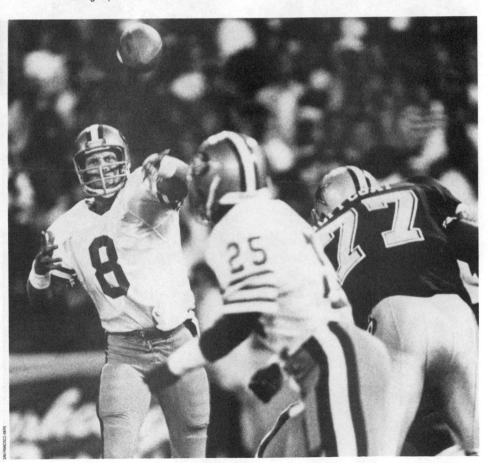

Quarterbacking the San Francisco 49ers, 1987

ROBBIE BOSCO

At the Punt, Pass & Kick competition, thirteen years old

"Is this the body of a wishbone quarterback?"

Setting up a run

BYU press book photo, 1984

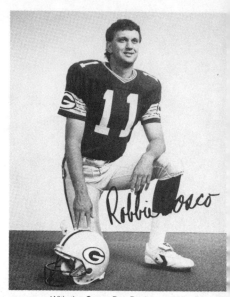

With the Green Bay Packers, 1988

Looking for a national championship, 1984

COACHES

LaVell Edwards

Ted Tollner

Mike Holmgren

Doug Scovil

JIM MCMAHON

"NOBODY DOES IT BETTER"
—Carly Simon, 1978

*H*e *was treading on the* delicate coach-player rela-tionship, so he put the question as diplomatically as he knew how.

"What *are* we doing?" he screamed.

"Giving up?"

BYU had dug itself a considerable hole in the 1980 Holiday Bowl. Southern Methodist University, with Craig James and Eric Dickerson trading off at running back, had run to a 38-19 lead early in the fourth quarter. BYU coach LaVell Edwards and his offensive coordinator, Doug Scovil, decided twenty-five thou-sand people heading for the San Diego Stadium exits couldn't be wrong. It was over. When a third-down play didn't work with BYU on its own forty-six-yard line, Edwards sent the punting team onto the field. In the meantime, quarterback Jim McMahon had al-ready huddled the offense. In the confusion BYU had twenty-two players on the field. Considering the way the game had gone, that seemed about right. Now it might be a fair fight.

McMahon called time-out and went to the sidelines. The mass exodus for the parking lot continued.
A sellout crowd of 50,214 had initially arrived to see
the SMU Mustangs play the BYU Cougars, an intriguing confrontation, it had seemed up front, between
a running team and a passing team. Now they had
seen enough.

McMahon pulled his chin strap off.

"Let's just quit right now!" he shouted. "If we punt
we lose!"

Edwards and Scovil exchanged a glance. They were
playing one of the best teams in the country—one of
the best teams money could buy, as it would turn out
after subsequent NCAA investigations. The Cougars
had been folded, spindled, and mutilated.

"So what do you suggest?" asked Edwards.

"That we don't punt," said McMahon.

He went back to midfield, waved the punting unit
off, and called an option play in the huddle. He could
go to either side with a pass, or he could run. The
Cougars needed two yards. He went to Clay Brown's
side with a pass—Brown had already caught two touchdown passes—and the tight end pulled it in twelve
yards away for the first down.

Maybe ten people sat back in their seats.

Ten plays later Scott Phillips plunged from one yard
out to end the drive with a touchdown. SMU's lead
was trimmed to 38-25. So far so good. The problem
was, SMU got the ball again. And James, who would
rush for 225 yards on twenty-three carries, picked up
where he'd left off, breaking loose for a forty-two-yard
touchdown run from scrimmage that brought the score
to 45-25 with 3:58 remaining.

This was not going to be easy, McMahon realized
as he again huddled up the BYU offense. Ray Scott,
the play-by-play announcer for Mizlou, the network
that was televising the game nationwide, had already

declared the game over. After James' touchdown he announced to what was left of his audience, "And for Brigham Young it turns out to be its third fruitless trip to the Holiday Bowl."

To this point in its history BYU was to bowl games what Sam Snead had been to the U. S. Open. Second place was the best BYU had done in the four bowl games they had played under the alias of Pass U. Getting there hadn't been most of the fun, it had been all the fun.

Such had the pressure been as the Cougars prepared for SMU. Coach LaVell Edwards, who believed bowl games should be a reward, was cutting himself no such slack this time. He secluded himself during the week in his suite at the San Diego Hilton, worrying. "This is a bowl game we *have* to win," he said.

McMahon's sentiment was the same. To direct BYU to its first-ever bowl win would cap his season-long, self-appointed crusade. A lot of students leave BYU to go on a mission. McMahon's mission had been to stay at BYU—and, as he put it, "break every record Marc Wilson ever set."

After earning WAC Offensive Player of the Year honors as a sophomore in 1978, when he alternated at quarterback with Wilson, McMahon had been red-shirted for the 1979 season. That hadn't been his choice. He had pleaded with the coaches to make it a competitive situation between himself and Wilson, a senior, for the top job—and may the best man win. "If he beats me I sit on the bench and lose a year of eligibility and that's it," McMahon had said. But he was vetoed by the coaches, who preferred the idea of stockpiling their quarterbacks for the next three seasons. He considered transferring, and contacted his high school coaches in San Jose for help in finding a new school. But then he reconsidered. For one thing, BYU was the best passing school in America. For another, he had something to prove — that he should never have been made to take a backseat to anyone.

During the 1979 season he had watched impatiently as Wilson and the Cougars won all eleven of their regular-season games and Wilson set eighteen NCAA records. The season's only blemish had come in the Holiday Bowl against Indiana when Brent Johnson's field goal at the buzzer missed wide to the left and BYU lost 38-37. It had been McMahon, striding the sidelines as a redshirt that evening, who had been the first on the field to console Johnson. He had put his arm around him and told him not to worry about it, those things happen. And they'd get them next year.

Only now, here it was, next year, and the Cougars were down by twenty with 3:58 left to play, and the TV announcer had already sent America to bed.

SAN JOSE, CALIFORNIA/ROY, UTAH
1959-1976

About the only nationality *not* represented on Maui Drive in East San Jose in the 1960s was Hawaiian.

Maui Drive, and the surrounding streets of Honolulu, Kauai and Oahu, had a lot of culture. You could find Japanese and Chicanos and blacks and Puerto Ricans and Samoans and Caucasians. There weren't any Vietnamese. Yet. A decade later, after Saigon had been renamed Ho Chi Minh City and those who resisted the Viet Cong had made their way to America, there would be. The Vietnamese proclaimed San Jose, with its moderate climate and small buildings, "Little Saigon" and settled in by the thousands.

But in 1961, when Jim and Roberta McMahon made a coast-to-coast move and transferred their family of six children — three boys followed by three girls — from Jersey City, New Jersey, to San Jose, Maui Drive was barely removed from the developer's blueprints. The masses were just starting to pour in. The McMahon

106

home on 3884 Maui was bordered on one side by prune orchards and on the other by the parking lot of Andrew Hill High School, where the kids would one day go to school — providing they made it that far.

Even from the start, it was not Mr. Rogers' neighborhood. You didn't go to school by bus, you went there by your fists. Especially if you were white and wore glasses and were scrawny — as Jimmy McMahon was. And more especially if you fought back.

Jimmy had help with his battles. He and his brother Mike were inseparable. Mike was eleven months older and they were always on the same side, except when they played one-on-one basketball in the backyard, where they would start with a game of twenty-one and end with a war. It was humorous, if you wanted to look at it that way. One minute they'd be walking home from Hellyer Elementary School, taking on a gang of blacks or Hispanics just to make it to the house. The next minute they'd be in the backyard trying to kill each other.

As rough as East San Jose was, it was also close to perfect as a sports incubator. There were well-organized Little Leagues in all the sports; there were, on the average, 363 days during the year when you could play outside; there were kids everywhere; and, if you needed them, there were plenty of heroes playing for the nearby San Francisco Giants, Oakland Raiders, and San Francisco 49ers.

For Jim and Mike, and, later, for their younger brother Danny, there was also their dad, Jim McMahon, Sr., who, when he wasn't holding down two jobs, was playing sports with them and coaching their teams. Jim McMahon wasn't as much of a stage parent as he was someone to play with. His boys loved sports, as he did, and they could play sports for free.

Jim McMahon was an East Coast person himself, born and raised in New Jersey. He had been a quarterback in high school, but he was far from the biggest kid on the team. They had given him number 1 for his jersey because a two-digit number wouldn't fit.

While based in Chicago with the U. S. Army, McMahon, Sr. had met his wife, Roberta, who had been born and raised in

Fresno, California. Roberta was in the service as well, where she excelled as an athlete on the army's championship volleyball team and as a catcher on the softball team.

They took a furlough in Chicago and were married, and after their army duty was over moved to New Jersey, where they lived until Jim got a job offer to work in the accounting department of a packaging company in San Jose.

Jim McMahon's chief form of discipline was to keep his sons off the streets by playing sports, and by playing them with a fervor. "If you're going to play, play to win," he told his three sons.

They took him literally. They wouldn't even let *him* win. They gave their old man no breaks. In the early years he would take on Mike and Jim in a game of football in the front yard. Then he recruited Danny for help. Then they had to give him a neighborhood kid to make it even.

This was when Mike and Jimmy were ten years old. They'd be playing football with their dad in the front yard. In the kitchen Roberta would hear screams and would yell out, "Don't hurt those boys!"

"Hurt those boys?" her husband would say. "They're hurting me!"

Off-the-field discipline was left to Roberta, whose athletic ability spilled over into her occasional showdowns with Jimmy, her feistiest. Many of the children who lived in the area roamed the streets day and night, but the McMahons had strict rules about that, and their mother was the enforcer. High on her list of favorite things were manners, clean rooms, and good grades. Because sports were what mattered to her boys most, she used them as bargaining tools. In high school she made Jim quit the basketball team for a few weeks one season when his grades slipped below the B level. That didn't just get Jimmy's attention but the attention of his coaches, too, who helped him find the library.

As moms go, she was no pushover.

As kids go, Jimmy was no Little Lord Fauntleroy.

He showed terrific diversification as a budding juvenile delinquent. As a youth, he did everything but burn down the school. He got caught for vandalizing the junior high—they recognized the graffiti as being in his handwriting. He slapped his classmates. He slapped his teachers. He put thumbtacks on chairs at school and tossed firecrackers during shop class. On his way home he had a favorite pastime of locking the gate to the school yard in front of a little crippled girl who was trying to get out. At thirteen he got drunk for the first time—at a Little League baseball picnic. And he was always sneaking off for a smoke.

His mother spent as much time at school as Jimmy did. They were both constantly in the principal's office.

He was not enamored by authority. His mother, for instance, would insist that Jimmy wear a jacket to school. They'd argue, she'd threaten to not let him go to football practice that night, he'd wear the jacket; but then, when he was safely away from home but still within his mother's view, he would take off the jacket and fling it in the bushes.

Jimmy didn't have a death wish, however. He didn't like to get in trouble when he didn't have to, which is how he almost lost his right eye. He was six when he tried to untie a lace on his gun holster with a fork. The fork slipped and punctured his eye. He was in a good deal of pain, but his father had the car at work and Jimmy didn't want to tell his mother what had happened because he was afraid she might wonder what he was doing with a fork and yell at him. He sat on a chair for six hours before he finally told her.

When they got to the hospital the doctors said he had severed the retina and it might be too late to save the eye.

They operated the next morning and then strapped Jimmy to a hospital bed for a week. After that they put him in a wheelchair and kept him another week. A model patient he wasn't. He organized a children's ward whiffle-ball game, stole the other kids' food, and, with very poor equilibrium, climbed onto the hospital roof to retrieve a whiffle ball he had hit through the window for a home-run. The nurses voted him least likely to succeed. They wanted to give him an early release. They wondered what he was like when he was *healthy*.

But the eye came around. Not completely, and not quickly, but it gradually improved. At first Jimmy had to wear thick dark glasses because his eye was extremely sensitive to light. But after a time he had to wear the glasses outdoors only, and partial vision returned.

The eye injury did not slow his sports pursuits. It did give him, as he would say later, a built-in excuse should he ever throw an interception. And the dark glasses would add to his mystique.

For the most part it was sports that kept Jimmy from becoming a felon at an early age. He didn't have time. There were still, even on the athletic courts, the occasional outbursts against authority. He was kicked off the baseball team when he was twelve for stealing cigarettes. Not only did the cigarettes belong to the coach, but the coach was his dad. There was the time in a Little League football game that he was dropped by a tackle after the whistle had blown the play dead. He picked up the ball, threw it at the player who had tackled him, and then reached up and slugged the referee who had not thrown a flag. His brother Mike had to finish at quarterback. Jimmy was thrown out of the game.

But sports, in the main, served as a positive motivator. He would do the dishes so he could play sports. He would go to class. He would *play* the game.

Jimmy was never the biggest kid on the block, or on his teams, and he didn't *look* like a quarterback. But from day one that was his position. His first Little League coach had a very objective way of choosing his quarterback. He'd line all the kids up and have them throw the football. Farthest throw won the job.

When Jimmy was ten he threw it sixty-five yards.

At Andrew Hill High School he became the first sophomore in the history of the school to start at quarterback. Jack Germaine, the head football coach, didn't care how old Jim was. "Best release I ever saw," was all he said when he named McMahon his starter.

"Normally, there can be real problems with a sophomore telling juniors and seniors what to do," said Germaine. "But nobody challenged Jim. He had this air about him during a game. He was all business. He wanted to win."

In his first high school start McMahon marched the Andrew Hill offense seventy-eight yards in the final 1:29 for a 13-7, come-from-behind win over Pioneer High School. He hit Lemuel Booth, a junior wide receiver, with the winning touchdown pass in the final seconds. An air of invincibility immediately started to grow around this little 5'7", 125-pound kid with glasses. When McMahon spoke in the huddle, his older teammates listened. When McMahon suggested a play on the sidelines, the coaches listened. Midway through the season, when a tackle separated McMahon's shoulder, everyone listened when he insisted that they just pop it back into place and get on with the game. An assistant coach straddled the shoulder and popped it back in. But it didn't hold. Jimmy couldn't play. He was out for several games, the arm hanging like a dishrag. Scar tissue eventually formed and allowed him to go on with the season, but the injury would come back to haunt him, both in college and in the NFL. Doctors would examine the shoulder, ask about its history, and invariably exclaim, "You did *what?*"

That's the way Jim McMahon was; that was the package. There wasn't a coach in the world who didn't know this was a rare athlete, which is why, in the spring of 1975, Jack Germaine felt as though he'd been hit by a truck when Jim McMahon, Sr., visited him on the Andrew Hill playing field.

"We're moving," said McMahon.

Germaine, a burly man with hands like hams—if Disney was casting a high school football coach, Jack Germaine could be the prototype—let his shoulders drop.

"Where?" he asked.

"Utah," said McMahon.

"Is that too far to commute?" asked the coach.

Years later, after the Vietnamese had taken over the bulk of the studentbody at Andrew Hill, and Germaine's entire football roster had dwindled to barely more than twenty players, he said of losing Jim McMahon in 1974: "It was like finding a golden nugget in the stream. Then it slips out of your hand . . . "

Germaine and the other coaches at Andrew Hill tried their best to talk McMahon's father into letting the two oldest boys, Mike and Jim, stay and finish what they'd started.

The coaches succeeded with Mike. He was coming into his senior year, and his parents agreed to let him live with the wrestling coach and remain behind in San Jose. Mike excelled in football, wrestling and baseball in his senior year, and was named Andrew Hill's Outstanding Senior Athlete.

Rick Alves, Jim's freshman coach at Andrew Hill, lobbied hard to have Jim stay with him. But his parents felt that two years was too long to have Jimmy away. Roberta didn't like him out of her sight for two minutes. His track record during his first sixteen years hadn't helped.

Like it or not, he was moving to Roy with his three sisters, his younger brother, and his parents. And even though Roberta had spent two years of her youth growing up in Ely, Nevada, and was a convert to the Mormon church, neither she nor any member of her family knew any more about Utah than they knew about Einstein's law of relativity.

Jimmy put off the move as long as possible, playing on a San Jose all-star baseball team until late in the summer. Meanwhile, Jim, Sr., had moved to Roy, where he not only scouted out a house for the family but scouted the football situation at Roy High School.

He found out the name of the head coach, Ernie Jacklin, and called him on the phone.

"What kind of offense do you run?" asked McMahon.

"The wishbone," said Jacklin.

"You might want to consider the pro-set after you've seen my son, Jimmy," said McMahon.

On the other end of the line Jacklin rolled his eyes. Another parent. From California.

At the Roy football practices—this was in August and two-a-days were going on—Jimmy's father watched from his car and discovered that the Royals already had not one but two returning starters at quarterback. Both were seniors. One, Rick Stonehocker, was the thrower and came in for passing plays. The other, Greg Pamphlock, was bigger and faster and was used for running plays.

"You've got two of them to beat out," McMahon told his son when he flew back to San Jose.

When Jimmy got to Roy he drove to the practice field himself and watched from the car. He drove back home. "If I can't play here, then I'm quitting," he said.

When he reported for practice the next day Jacklin had forgotten about the phone call and about changing to the pro-set, and he put his California move-in as the third-team quarterback, where he stayed until the first intrasquad scrimmage a week later. Running the wishbone offense against the first-team defense, McMahon's third-stringers outscored both the first- and second-team offenses. Just like that, Roy had a new quarterback.

Jacklin had seen the same thing Germaine had seen before him. He switched to the pro-set by the middle of the 1975 season. In the next two seasons Roy, a new school devoid of much football tradition, would win nineteen games and lose only three.

It was while at Roy that McMahon started to think seriously about making sports his career. He still had his occasional run-ins with authority. Once, when the basketball coach told him to stop lifting weights (for football) or he couldn't play on the basketball team, Jim responded by flinging his uniform at the coach. The coach reconsidered. McMahon was his starting guard.

But mostly, McMahon got people's attention because of what he was doing in one sport or another. Some examples:

His junior year he was playing for Roy against Cottonwood High School in the Utah Class 4-A baseball championships in Salt Lake City. Cottonwood was undefeated in the double-elimination tournament and needed the win for the title. A Roy win, on the other hand, would give each team one loss and set up more games. Entering the bottom of the ninth inning Cottonwood led 8-4. Roy loaded the bases. There was one out when McMahon came to the plate. He took a look at one pitch, a strike, and lifted the next pitch over the left-field wall for a grand-slam home run that set up a 9-8 Roy win.

During McMahon's senior year, Roy was playing a basketball game against Springville High when Springville's Scott Phillips — who would later be McMahon's teammate on the BYU football team — dived for a ball going out-of-bounds. He grabbed the ball and threw it at McMahon's legs so it would bounce off him.

McMahon reached down, caught the ball at his ankles, and put it in the basket to give Roy a one-point win.

There were other stories, all similar, and college recruiters in three sports began to come around. The Boston Red Sox sent a scout. Jimmy McMahon was in demand.

Utah State University basketball coach Dutch Belnap wanted Jimmy badly, and told him he could play both football and basketball for the Aggies. But when McMahon told Belnap he also wanted to play baseball, Belnap had a problem. Utah State didn't have a baseball team.

College coaches in pursuit of a recruit, however, are nothing if not inventive. Belnap came up with a solution. He had once been general manager of the Ogden Dodgers of the Pioneer League when Tommy Lasorda was the team's field manager. Belnap called Lasorda, who in turn called the McMahon home in Roy. Jim McMahon, Sr., who took the phone, thought it was a joke. Why was the manager of the Los Angeles Dodgers calling him? Then he understood when Lasorda said, "I've got a daughter going to Utah State. I like the school a lot, and if you'd like to play baseball in the summer there's a spot in the Dodger organization for you."

Jimmy took his recruiting visit to Utah State. He also visited Oklahoma State and Nebraska—both were interested in him for football—and Boise State and Nevada-Las Vegas, and when BYU and the University of Utah came to talk, he listened. In the back of his dreams he hoped to hear from Notre Dame—he was a Catholic, that was his father's religion—for whom he would have dropped everything and everybody.

But the Irish never called, so in the end, on letter-of-intent-signing day, it came to this: He wanted to play football and baseball, and he wanted to go to a school where they threw the football.

He had three recruiters at his home—one each from Nevada-Las Vegas, Utah State, and BYU—when the signing hour came. He kept them on hold in the front room for an hour and a half. He wasn't trying to be rude, he just didn't know which one to choose.

Finally he said, "I think I'll be a Cougar."

BYU assistant coach Garth Hall asked if he could use the

phone. He called the office and said, "I think we got Jim Mc-Mahon."

When it got right down to it, McMahon chose BYU to please his parents. The Cougars were their choice. Roberta wanted him at a school that might keep him in control. She had stayed awake nights imagining her son in Las Vegas for four years. Jim, Sr. wanted his son at a major league program where he could play either football or baseball and become the star he was convinced his son was destined to be. When Jimmy had leaned toward Boise State for a while, because they were agreeable to a dual football/baseball deal, Jim McMahon said, "Not a big enough school for Jimmy's talents." He felt the same way about Utah State.

But wherever his son went, Jim, Sr. didn't want him to sit on the bench. When the McMahons negotiated with BYU, he asked LaVell Edwards for his personal guarantee that Jimmy, as a freshman, would be given every opportunity to contend for the starting quarterback position. The fact that Gifford Nielsen, home-grown in Provo, was coming into his senior season as a preseason All-American didn't matter. He told the BYU football coach the same thing he'd told the Roy football coach two years before: "I'm telling you, my kid can play."

1977-1978

The first time Dr. Brent Pratley met Jim McMahon was in Corvallis, Oregon, in a rainstorm. Pratley, the new BYU team surgeon, and McMahon were standing on the sidelines as BYU opened the 1978 football season at Oregon State.

"Who are you?" asked Pratley.

"I'm the quarterback," said McMahon.

"They already have one," said Pratley.

"Oh," said McMahon. "I hadn't noticed."

"I'm also the punter," said McMahon.

"Not a good job on a day like this," said Pratley. "I'll bet you fifty bucks you couldn't kick one of those soggy balls thirty yards."

"You're on," said McMahon, who at that point was sent into the game.

115

He got off a forty-seven-yard punt.

As he trotted off the field, Pratley reached into his pocket. "Naw, put it away," said McMahon. "It wasn't a fair bet."

From this exchange developed a strong relationship between the doctor and the quarterback. "Brent Pratley was like a second father to me," McMahon would later say. It was Pratley's advice that would influence McMahon's future at BYU more than any other.

Since the first time he had put on a BYU uniform the year before, McMahon had been the Cougars' first-team punter. He played only a few downs at quarterback. As the number-four quarterback as a freshman he had thrown sixteen passes and completed ten in fourth-quarter, mop-up work. He watched as a third-year sophomore, Marc Wilson, took over for the injured All-American Gifford Nielsen and was named all-WAC in the process. The only thing McMahon got to do was punt—fifty-five times for a 39.3 average, including two punts of fifty-four yards. That and pout. He hadn't just thought he was better than Wilson, but Nielsen, too.

So had his father, who pushed for the "equal opportunity" clause during the recruiting of his phenomenal—if he did say so himself—son. Jim McMahon, Sr. traveled to Oregon State to see the first game of the 1978 season, and when Wilson got off to a slow and soggy start—completing just fifteen of thirty-eight passes for 193 yards with three interceptions in a bare 10-6 win—his concern that the "equal opportunity" clause had not been honored got the best of him. He stormed into the locker room after the game to tell the coaches what he thought. Jimmy intervened and escorted the senior McMahon back out in the rain to cool off.

Football wasn't the only area where McMahon was having difficulty at Brigham Young University. The sign at the school's entrance proclaimed "The World Is Our Campus," but he personally found a world of difference between life at BYU and elsewhere.

It was nothing like East San Jose, or even Roy, for that matter. This was a place that thought Coca Cola was evil. McMahon fit into the BYU mainstream like a rainbow trout in salt water. For two years he fought a head wind. As an incoming freshman he had agreed to abide by the school's honor code—a code that required students to abstain from drugs, alcohol and tobacco, cheating, and premarital sex, and demanded that they in general observe high moral standards, including the golden rule. But as one teacher observed after McMahon's freshman year, "He had his fingers crossed."

He didn't rob any banks or rape any women or do anything else that would make either the ten o'clock news or the police blotter downtown. But he was nonetheless turned in for numerous honor code violations.

McMahon was seen drinking beer on the municipal golf course in Provo. He had loud parties in his apartment. He got into fights. He and the standards office had an ongoing adversarial relationship. McMahon noticed cars following him around town. He felt uncomfortable in Provo. He returned to Roy often and spent time with his brother Mike, who was on a wrestling scholarship at Weber State College in Ogden. During his first three years at BYU, McMahon actually spent more time in Ogden, where he engaged in a great deal more social activity than in Provo and got in a great deal less trouble.

Complaints about McMahon were a regular thing with Edwards, who tended to take them in stride. One day he got three calls from anonymous callers, each claiming they had seen McMahon the previous Friday night buying beer at a local 7-11. They were all different 7-11s. And McMahon had been in Ogden all weekend.

Still, he was not completely innocent, nor did he pretend to be. Once, after he became famous and was being interviewed by the *Los Angeles Times*, he made a point of chewing tobacco during the interview. This small detail neither eluded the reporter, who included it in his article the next morning, nor the dozens of people who sent copies of the article to the BYU standards office.

McMahon tended to stay away from the orthodox at BYU. He roomed for a time with Gym Kimball, a free-spirited quarterback from Salt Lake City who later transferred to Utah State. His best friend, aside from Pratley, was Danny Plater, a wide receiver on the football team from Nevada. His final year he lived in the basement of the home of Carl Severe, an avid BYU booster and a McMahon sympathizer.

McMahon's closest confidant was his girlfriend, Nancy Daines. They met when both were freshmen and Nancy, living in the dorms, asked Jim to a girls'-choice dance. Nancy had grown up in the San Carlos area near San Francisco not far from where Jim had been raised in San Jose. She was the daughter of a stake president who had come to BYU because it was her Church's school. Jim was a Catholic who wished he was at Notre Dame. They hit it off anyway (as the standards office duly noted). Four years later they would be married.

It wasn't easy being Jim McMahon's girlfriend at BYU. Nancy noticed cars following her, too, and assumed they were from standards. When Jim was at her apartment there would sometimes be people sitting in cars parked across the street. Bothered by the attention, after three years she stopped attending BYU and enrolled in a beauty school.

As a student-athlete, McMahon downplayed the student part. He didn't go to BYU to go to class, he went to play football. Classwork was a necessary evil. During his third year, when he redshirted, he barely took any classes. The twelve hours he took the fall of his senior year all ended up as incompletes. Still, with a natural intelligence and the need to complete enough hours each semester to stay eligible for football, by the time he'd thrown his last pass as a Cougar in the Holiday Bowl of 1981, he was within one semester of graduating.

In spite of the Stalag 13 atmosphere McMahon found confining, there was nonetheless a lot of brilliant football at BYU. It kept him around, not to mention challenged. It wasn't long after he enrolled that he gave up the idea of playing baseball. He played briefly on the BYU junior varsity team his freshman year, but then hurt his arm. After that, he didn't have the time. It was a full-time job trying to win the quarterback position.

While the standards office was watching everything he did, or at least giving it the old college try, the football coaches barely gave him a look. When Nielsen had gone down with a broken knee in 1977, quarterback coach Doug Scovil hadn't even considered McMahon as a replacement.

But in 1978 Scovil had gone to the NFL, and the new quarterback coach, Wally English, had a different point of view—one largely shaped by an incident that happened early during August workouts.

English had introduced a new rollout play that called for the quarterback to pass to the tight end. When Marc Wilson, the incumbent starting quarterback, tried the play, he threw instead to the wide receiver. English slammed down his clipboard.

"Run the play right," he said. So they lined up again, and again Wilson threw to the wide receiver.

Now English was irate. He called for the number-two quarterback, McMahon.

McMahon ran the play—and threw to the wide receiver.

English blew up.

McMahon blew up back. He told English he had thrown to the wide receiver because the tight end was getting tackled every time down field by the linebacker, that if he was watching he'd have seen it himself, and, furthermore, it was a stupid play and would never work.

In the film room the next day, the films exonerated McMahon. The linebacker *had* been taking the tight end out of the play. English apologized to McMahon. Then he turned to Wilson and told him he should have stuck up for himself.

From then on, McMahon was English's man. The coach did not like Wilson's introverted style. He liked McMahon's leadership.

The feeling wasn't mutual. After their one and only season together in 1978, McMahon said, "Wally English was the worst football coach I ever played for, on any level, anywhere, ever."

Still, McMahon thrived, to a point. Wilson turned progressively into a mental basket case, and midway through the sixth game of the season, when the Cougars, with a so-so 3-2 record, went back to Oregon, this time to play the University of Oregon in Eugene, McMahon won the starting job. In the third quarter he was sent in to replace Wilson, who to that point had completed ten of twenty-one passes for two interceptions and just eighty-one yards. BYU had scored a mere three points as a result, to Oregon's sixteen.

McMahon went ten of nineteen the rest of the way for 204 yards and one touchdown pass that won the game, 17-16.

He got his first official start in the next game, against UTEP in Provo, and directed a 44-0 win. Then, in successive WAC games against Wyoming and San Diego State, he was in charge of 48-14 and 21-3 wins that clinched the WAC title and a first-ever Holiday Bowl berth for the Cougars—and clinched for McMahon the WAC Offensive Player of the Year award.

In the tenth game, against Utah, McMahon suffered his first defeat as a collegiate starter. BYU's 16-0 halftime lead slipped away to a 23-22 loss. In the second half McMahon tripped over his own foot and severely strained his left knee. That put him on crutches and put Wilson back in the quarterback business.

In games against Hawaii and Nevada-Las Vegas (in Japan) Wilson directed two wins. But Edwards told McMahon he was still the starter, and as long as the tendonitis in his knee cleared up he would start in the Holiday Bowl against Navy.

At least that's the way McMahon heard it.

But when the team arrived in San Diego to prepare for the Navy game, Edwards told English to tell McMahon that Wilson would start the game.

English went to McMahon's room at the San Diego Hilton and gave him the news.

McMahon told English what he thought of the decision, and then went to find Edwards and tell *him* what he thought. He found the coach standing in front of the Hilton swimming pool, which is in the center of the lobby area and a very public place.

McMahon got to the point quickly.

"You lied to me!" he accused. "You said I'd start this game."

Edwards said he didn't remember giving any guarantees.

McMahon said he did, and stomped off.

He ended up playing more than half the Holiday Bowl game anyway. He took over for Wilson in the second quarter and passed for one touchdown and ran for another. But the BYU offense was as out of sync as the coaching staff, and thirteen unanswered Navy points in the fourth quarter gave the Midshipmen a 23-16 win.

McMahon returned to Provo to have his knee operated on and to ponder his future. He wasn't sure he wanted it to include BYU.

After the surgery had been performed to repair the tendonitis, he took a personal inventory: He had a cast on his left leg; he'd caught the chicken pox in the hospital; he had lost his starting quarterback job; one of his coaches was an idiot and the other had lied to him; he was at the top of the standards office's most-wanted list; and now there was talk that BYU was thinking about redshirting him for the 1979 season.

He got on the phone and contacted Rick Alves and Jack Germaine, his high school coaches in San Jose, and asked them to check with Bay Area colleges that might be interested in his services. He also made inquiries to Weber State.

When Brent Pratley, who had performed the knee surgery, came by his hospital room, McMahon told him all he wanted were his crutches and a road map.

"I'm out of here," he said. "Life's too short."

Pratley suggested that maybe he should think about it, that there were a lot of good reasons for staying.

"Name one," said McMahon.

"You can be the punter."

"Name another."

Pratley went down his list. Among other things McMahon should consider, Pratley said, was that there was no better place to learn the passing game than BYU. If you wanted to be a nuclear scientist you went to M.I.T. If you wanted to be a quarterback you went to BYU. Why go somewhere else and start over again? He told him he could spend his redshirt year at his house if he wanted. Then he said something that really got McMahon's attention.

"Wouldn't there be some satisfaction in rising above it all and rubbing it in their faces?"

Now *that* made sense.

1979

Redshirt seasons move along with all the speed of a glacier, and so it went for Jim McMahon in 1979. He ran the scout teams in practice, went to class, and spent most weekends in Ogden. The fact that Wilson was having phenomenal success didn't hurry the process. Wilson became the nation's undisputed top quarterback. He was the passing leader and the total offense leader. He set eighteen NCAA records and was a unanimous All-American. He won a new car in Alabama. He was on Bob Hope's Christmas special with the AP All-America team. And he was an NFL first-round draft choice.

All the while McMahon knew in his own mind that there was one college football player in America who was better:

Himself.

"Whatever he's done," he told Nancy, "I'll do it better."

1980

After more than a year of waiting and plotting and planning, of devising ways of rubbing it in everyone's faces, Jim McMahon took the field for his opening performance in 1980 and lost to New Mexico.

He was eleven of twenty-five as the Lobos won 25-21 in Albuquerque. McMahon threw one interception and passed for just 147 yards. Subtract his minus forty-four yards rushing and he had just 103 yards total offense. He also punted twice, for thirty-one and twenty-four yards. The Cougars had lost ugly. He'd lost ugly. As debuts by aspiring Heisman Trophy winners go—McMahon had added that modest goal to his list—it was not promising.

It was also the best loss BYU ever had.

New Mexico had had all summer to get ready for the Cougars,

and the Lobos had not loitered. They studied every BYU game film from the 1979 season, when the Cougars won by an average score of 39-9, and came to a realization that no single defense worked consistently against the BYU passing system. Certainly San Diego State's full-scale blitz hadn't worked, and neither had other game-long gambles. The Lobos masterminded a changeable defense. On one play they would overload the right side and blitz from there. On the next play they would overload the left. On some plays they would drop seven or eight defenders back into the zones. They stunted on every down. The idea was to confuse and destroy.

And it worked. BYU's offensive line short-circuited in the face of all this organized chaos. McMahon had to scramble constantly and throw off-balance. It had taken the Lobos all summer to get ready, but theirs was the best answer a defense had yet devised to stop BYU at the pass.

When the Cougars returned to Provo, Roger French barricaded himself in his office and didn't come out for days. French was BYU's new offensive line coach in 1980, just hired from the University of Wisconsin, where he had been the defensive coordinator. Prior to that he had coached the offensive line at the University of Minnesota. French was a coach in the Doug Scovil mold. He didn't like football, he *loved* football. A challenge such as the one the Lobos had just thrown at him piqued his competitive nature. In the days and nights thereafter he came up with a new pass-blocking package for the offensive line, devising a series of calls that could be adapted to any formation a defense might try.

In its own way, what Roger French drew up for the offensive line was as revolutionary as anything Dewey Warren or Doug Scovil had ever invented.

Under French's direction, BYU's offensive line became the state of the art in pass blocking. The coach never quit tinkering. He tried anything and everything. He nudged as close as possible to that gray area between holding and not holding. For a while he had his linemen wear gloves the same color as the opposition's jerseys — a concept not unlike wearing camouflage clothing to blend in with the jungle.

123

Before French, Dave Kragthorpe, Edwards' original offensive coordinator in 1972 and later the assistant head coach in charge of the offensive line, had started BYU on its way to sophisticated pass blocking. After the 1979 season, Kragthorpe took his knowledge of the passing game with him to Idaho State, where in 1981 he used it to win a Division I-AA national championship.

Both French and McMahon were better prepared for their second try. In game two, BYU rebounded with a 35-11 win over San Diego State in which McMahon threw four touchdown passes for 373 yards. Even while earning all-WAC honors as a sophomore he hadn't had a day as smooth as this. He had thrown only six touchdown passes the entire 1978 season.

But it was back to Doug Scovil's system now, and as it had been with Nielsen and Wilson, so it was with McMahon. Every day Scovil and McMahon had their hour meeting. McMahon learned the gospel-according-to-Scovil, to wit: There are only eleven defense people, and they have to cover certain areas. Where they can't cover, that's where you exploit. Nothing fancy. Nothing extravagant.

"We had seven or eight unselfish white boys who could run routes and get open," McMahon said. "That was enough. They knew they'd get the ball. Plus, there was great protection."

Spurred in part by the rusty beginning at New Mexico, McMahon's regimen took on *Rocky* proportions. He spent as much time in the weight room as the linemen. He turned an average arm into a strong arm. He could run the forty-yard dash as fast as most running backs, in the 4.5 range. And in practice he was a perfectionist. During seven-on-seven scrimmages he would regularly complete 90 percent of his passes — and this against a defense that knew what he was going to do.

The only place he didn't linger was in the film room, where he used his photographic memory for quick studies. He could pick out defenses in a hurry. Either on film or on the field.

As unpopular as he was with the standards office, McMahon was popular with his teammates. Unlike Wilson (and like Nielsen and Sheide), he was one of them; one of the guys. He wasn't just good at football, he enjoyed playing the game. That rubbed off onto the other players. And to further his stature he occasionally gave the coaches some flak—always a good way to endear yourself to teammates.

At practice McMahon had a tendency toward colorful language. Swearing was his way of venting frustration, and he usually had a lot of frustration. During his junior year, word got back to the school administration that McMahon was not exactly sounding like a missionary during practice, and neither was the rest of the team. Dallin Oaks, the school president, asked Edwards to clean up the language.

Edwards pulled McMahon aside before practice and told him to watch his mouth. McMahon said he'd try. But old habits die hard, and finally, after about a third of the practice, Edwards blew his whistle.

"No more swearing!" he shouted.

McMahon made it maybe five more minutes.

A defensive back gave a hard shot to Danny Plater and a fight broke out. McMahon looked on in disgust and then swore, half to himself. But his timing was bad. Edwards was standing directly behind him, and he was not pleased.

The coach grabbed McMahon by his face mask and told him to hit the showers.

McMahon turned, looked at Edwards, and let go with a familiar expletive.

That was his parting shot.

There's nothing like a showdown between a head coach and his star quarterback to get a team's interest. The players were divided as to what would happen. There were those who thought McMahon would be suspended, at least for one game. And there were those who thought McMahon would call Edwards and apologize.

Neither of which happened. What did happen was that Edwards called McMahon at his apartment later that day. He called him several times, in fact. But McMahon told Nancy, who answered the phone, to tell him he wasn't there. Later in the evening, McMahon got in his car, an old Plymouth Duster, and drove to

Edwards' house. They talked, shook hands, and agreed to get back to normal. Whatever that was.

The only time football life was ever dull for McMahon was during the second half on Saturdays, when he spent most of his time sitting on the bench. After San Diego State fell 35-11, and Wisconsin 28-3, and Long Beach State 41-25, things really got lopsided. Wyoming lost 52-17, and Utah State scored forty-six points and still lost, 70-46. McMahon sat down with an NCAA record 342 yards passing in the first half against Utah State (there went one of Wilson's records). But in the second half the Aggies, trailing 64-24, scored eighteen unanswered points and McMahon, who had already thrown six touchdown passes, came back in to run for one more touchdown and secure the win.

There was a downside to the Aggie outburst, however. During the game McMahon reinjured his right shoulder, the one that had been custom set by the assistant coach his sophomore year at Andrew Hill High School. By the time the 6-0 Cougars arrived in Hawaii for a game against a Rainbow Warrior team that was expected to challenge BYU for the conference title, their starting quarterback couldn't lift his arm.

During pregame practices on the field at Iolani High School in Honolulu the Cougars, in an effort to keep McMahon's condition a secret, put McMahon's jersey on Gym Kimball. They weren't sure McMahon would be able to play. Pratley had examined the shoulder in Provo and had sent McMahon to Hawaii by way of Los Angeles, where orthopedic specialists Frank Jobe and Bob Kerlan gave a further examination. Forty-eight hours before the game, McMahon was given a steroid injection in the bursa. For good measure, he found an acupuncturist in Honolulu who also gave him treatment. By game time, either the steroids or the acupuncture, or both, had worked. McMahon could move his shoulder.

In a game much closer than the final score of 34-7 indicated, McMahon was pressed into full-time duty. He ran sixty-eight plays — nearly twice as many as normal — and threw sixty passes, the second highest total of his career. He completed thirty-one for two touchdowns, but he also threw three interceptions. He

126

had to bail himself out of a few tight spots as a result, including once when he was about to be tackled for a loss on a fourth-down play and quickly punted the ball thirty-one yards with his left foot.

For his performance, McMahon was named *Sports Illustrated*'s Back of the Week, although the magazine failed to note perhaps the most athletic move of his Hawaiian stay. That came one night at the Princess Kaiulani Hotel. McMahon wanted to visit whoever was staying in the room below his. He was on the twenty-fourth floor. To get to the twenty-third floor, he swung over the railing on the balcony and dropped below. So far so good. But no one was home. So he grabbed the railing above him and swung back up.

The next morning, when McMahon had a much clearer head, Plater, his roommate, walked him to the window and showed him what he had done the night before. "I *am* crazy," said McMahon.

Sports Illustrated showed up in Provo the next week for more McMahontics. His shoulder had made an amazing recovery, much to the disappointment of the UTEP Miners, who were grateful when McMahon was finally benched with 6:16 to play—in the second quarter. At the time the score was 42-0. By game's end it was 83-7. McMahon had thrown for six touchdowns in the early going and 372 yards—an NCAA first-half passing record that eclipsed the 342 yards he had thrown against Utah State. He was breaking every record, all right, including his own.

In the resulting *Sports Illustrated* article, the attention was not only on McMahon, but on Scovil, who, it was coming to light, had not only coached Staubach at Navy, but had now developed at BYU the Nielsen-Wilson-McMahon line. Scovil was given a new nickname—"Bombs Away Scovil"—and it was his picture that ran in the article.

By season's end Scovil would be hired away from BYU, this time for good, by San Diego State. And probably just in time. His increasing notoriety as the genius behind the Cougars' passing game was creating unrest among Edwards' coaching staff and with Edwards himself, who in earlier days had gotten along well with Scovil. But now egos were getting in the way.

None of it touched McMahon. To get ready for his first Holiday Bowl start and to wind up the regular season he beat Utah 56-6 and Nevada-Las Vegas 54-14. After losing to New Mexico to open the season, BYU won eleven straight games and scored 539 points for an average weekly win of 49-16. McMahon had thrown for more than three hundred yards every game, and for over four hundred yards four times.

During the December lull between the end of the regular season and the bowl games, record-keepers at NCAA headquarters in Kansas collected McMahon's statistics and went underground.

When they emerged they had given him credit for thirty-four NCAA records, and had ranked him as the most prolific and efficient college quarterback ever. No one had ever thrown for 4,571 yards before — that smashed the previous mark of 3,720 yards set by Wilson the year before. And no one had ever accumulated a season-long passing efficiency rating of 176.9 points — a figure that broke the fourteen-year NCAA record of 172.6 set by Tulsa's Jerry Rhome in 1966.

No one, for that matter, had ever thrown forty-seven touchdown passes in a single season, or averaged 10.27 yards per play, or had eleven straight three-hundred-yard passing games, or thrown as few as eighteen interceptions in 445 attempts.

Jim Van Valkenburg, the NCAA director of statistics and a man who goes by the book, waxed apoplectic. "What Jim McMahon did is comparable to what Babe Ruth did in baseball," said Van Valkenburg. "No quarterback in the history of college football has had a season like it. Ever."

McMahon assumed that included Marc Wilson.

Now all that remained was a challenge that had eluded every other quarterback in BYU history, not to mention every other Cougar football team. Could he get BYU a win in a bowl game?

HOLIDAY BOWL III

BYU came into the 1980 Holiday Bowl ranked fifteenth in the country. Its opponent, Southern Methodist University, was ranked nineteenth. Technically that made the Cougars the favorite. But BYU had to drag along the lead weight of having never won a bowl game, and SMU was a young team on the rise. The Mustangs had the two best running backs in the Southwest Conference, even if Craig James and Eric Dickerson were only sophomores. And time (and the NFL) would verify that the James/Dickerson tandem was as formidable as any pair of running backs in the modern era of college football. Beyond that, the Mustangs were loaded with other NFL-bound players. Defensive tackle Michael Carter was on his way to an Olympic medal in the shot put and a career with the San Francisco 49ers after that.

In 1980 the sophomore-laden Mustangs weren't sure just how good they were. But after three quarters of toying with the best from the Western Athletic Conference, they were getting a better idea. By the end of the third quarter coach Ron Meyer began substituting liberally, giving his reserves a taste of the good bowl life. In the press box Holiday Bowl officials were working toward an early finish, collecting MVP ballots from sportswriters. James, with 225 yards on the ground, was the easy winner on offense. Carter, with five unassisted tackles and two sacks, was the easy winner on defense.

But out on the field, McMahon hadn't yet given his concession speech. He had played a horrible first half, by his standards, and had looked like anything but the Babe Ruth of college football. Now all the numbers from the regular season were like points being erased off a pinball machine. The Cougars were being manhandled by SMU. They'd be lucky if they were ever ranked again.

After James' touchdown had given SMU its 45-25 lead, McMahon was fortunate Dallin Oaks wasn't within earshot. Or vice versa.

It wasn't the bowl game now, or anything to do with Marc Wilson. Jim McMahon just hated to lose.

So did any number of BYU fans around the country. James' touchdown run had sent them in a variety of directions, all of them away from this sad scene. Those watching on television switched to the late movie or went to bed. Those in Jack Murphy Stadium were on their way to the parking lot. The next morning, thousands of BYU fans would awake convinced that BYU had blown another one.

With 3:58 on the game clock McMahon knew he had to fast-forward things. He marched the Cougars seventy-two yards in 2:31 and ended the drive with a fifteen-yard touchdown pass to Matt Braga. The two-point PAT failed.

45-31.

Next came an onside kick, football's version of pulling the goalie.

It worked. BYU's Todd Shell recovered at the fifty-yard line.

Four plays later Scott Phillips completed a thirty-four-second drive with a one-yard touchdown plunge, then took a two-point PAT pass from McMahon.

45-39.

Another onside kick. Unsuccessful.

Now SMU could run out the clock. But Dickerson—he was back, along with all the Mustang regulars—couldn't get around Redd and Bill Schoepflin on the corner on a third-down run. With a fourth-and-four on the BYU forty-three-yard line, SMU had to punt. The Mustangs let the twenty-five-second clock expire and, with eighteen seconds left, took the resultant five-yard, delay-of-game penalty. Then they punted. Or tried to.

Schoepflin blocked the punt.

BYU had the ball back, at the SMU forty-one-yard line.

Thirteen seconds left.

Cars outside the stadium on Friars Road came to a standstill. Some tried to turn around to get back to the stadium in time.

McMahon threw to Brown. Incomplete.

McMahon threw deep down the right side to Lloyd Jones. Incomplete.

Three seconds left. The ball was still on the SMU forty-one-yard line. There was time for one pass.

Doug Scovil, in his last official call for BYU, sent in the play. "Save the Game" was its name. It was a play they'd fooled around with at the close of every week's practice, for laughs more than anything else; the kind of play you draw up in the sand at the beach with the receivers all converging in the end zone and the quarterback throwing it as high and far as he possibly can.

"Save the Game," said McMahon in the huddle.

Tight end Clay Brown was the primary receiver. His assignment was the middle of the end zone. At the hike of the ball he headed there. He had never been so popular. In the end zone four SMU players surrounded him. Back at the fifty-yard line, where he'd backpedaled in the pocket, McMahon could barely see the end zone through the late night mist.

He threw a high, arching spiral.

Brown could see it coming. So could his escorts. They went up. As they were coming down he went up.

The ball hit him in his favorite place. His hands.

Touchdown.

As Edwards, his head down, started to walk off the field, Scovil pulled him back.

"Hey," he said, "it worked."

Kurt Gunther was ushered onto the field, where he kicked the extra point with no time on the clock to give BYU a 46-45 win.

In tears, James and Carter came to midfield to accept their trophies. BYU picked up its trophy, the one for first place.

In the locker room, a team manager thrust a football at McMahon for his autograph. He tried to sign his name, but his hand was shaking too badly.

1981

Ted Tollner, the newly appointed quarterback coach at BYU, asked Jim McMahon to come into his office and shut the door.

Tollner had most recently been a coach at San Diego State, where he had been in charge of the offense. But after the Aztecs went 4-8 in 1980, they fired head coach Claude Gilbert and replaced him with Doug Scovil. Now Tollner was taking Scovil's place at BYU. It was "as the world turns" in college football coaching.

"The first thing I want to know," he said to McMahon, "is about this place. What's it like here at BYU?"

McMahon smiled.

"Watch your back," he said.

"The second thing I want to know," Tollner said, "is how you run your offense. We couldn't beat you." (San Diego State had lost to BYU by 35-11, 63-14, and 21-3 scores the past three seasons.) "I'm not going to try to change a thing."

"Smart coach," said McMahon.

They rode off into the sunset that way. Tollner, who had coached quarterbacks Jesse Freitas and Craig Penrose to NCAA passing championships at San Diego State, knew what he had inherited. He had inherited, as it would turn out, a quarterback and an offense that would land him the head coaching job at the University of Southern California the next season. When he looked at Scovil's playbook after he arrived — he only wished he'd had that opportunity the year before — he felt like the Germans when Einstein finally showed them how he made the bomb. "As innovative as any offense in college," he said. "It's effective because it's sound. It's an execution-pass offense, not a trick-'em pass offense."

For all their rapport, McMahon still liked to test the new coach. He'd look bored in the film room, as though he was dozing off, and Tollner would hit him with a question. "I never caught him, not once," said Tollner. "He could recognize coverages *that* fast. He didn't have to think, he went by instinct. He knew where everyone was supposed to go, what their routes were, and what they were supposed to do. If a guy wasn't running the right route, he'd tell him, and in language that would get his teammate's attention. But he was hard on himself, too. The players knew that. They knew he was playing as hard as he could, all the time."

The fall of 1981 was a time of football tranquility for McMahon at BYU. The hassles with standards continued. They caught him drinking beer. They caught him chewing tobacco. He was observed throwing clubs on the golf course. After McMahon was quoted on television that "BYU was no bed of roses," the student newspaper, *The Daily Universe*, came out with a cartoon showing McMahon tangled in a rosebush — an odd bit of journalism. How many college newspapers run editorial cartoons critical of their star quarterback? Then again, how many star quarterbacks publicly ridicule their school, as McMahon was doing in an increasing number of media interviews nationwide?

He had been decorated for his 1980 performance — a performance unprecedented in the history of college football quarterbacking. But not proportionately. He hadn't even been that year's consensus first-team All-American — an honor that went to Purdue's Mark Herrmann. In the Heisman Trophy balloting he was fifth, behind South Carolina's George Rogers, the nation's leading rusher that season; Pittsburgh defensive end Hugh Green; Georgia freshman running back Herschel Walker; and Herrmann.

For 1981 his goal was to win the Heisman Trophy. BYU started its "McMahon for Heisman" campaign in the late summer when associate sports information director Ralph Zobell found an old football uniform and shoes and dressed McMahon in them. He took photographs of him in a pose identical to the Heisman Trophy bust and sent the pictures to Heisman voters around the country. The race was on.

McMahon's penchant for perfection was, if anything, intensified. He didn't dwell on what he'd done already. He never had been the kind of athlete who was satisfied. Whenever he talked to his brother or dad after games, which he usually did, it was always, "I could have done better," and "that stupid interception." He remembered the interceptions more than the touchdowns, the incompletes more than the completes.

The 1981 season resumed where 1980 left off. In the first three games, all easy wins over Long Beach State, Air Force and UTEP, McMahon threw eight touchdown passes, completed 67 percent of his passes, and had only two interceptions. The country's best quarterback grew more and more confident. During the Air Force game, weary of hearing Falcon linebacker Mike France's constant taunts, he looked up while calling out his count and made a curious kind of audible. "I'm tired of your yelling," he said to France. "This one's coming right over you." Then he completed a pass over France's head to Dan Plater.

McMahon was cruising into game four in Boulder against the University of Colorado when a prediction he'd made in August was resurrected by the newspapers. McMahon had been asked during the WAC skywriters preseason tour about playing Colorado, a Big 8 school with a proud football tradition that had fallen on tough times in recent years.

"Oklahoma rushed for eight hundred yards against them in 1980," said McMahon. "We won't rush for eight hundred yards, but I'd like to throw for eight hundred, and I think I can."

The comment was turned into wallpaper that covered the Colorado locker room walls. When the Cougar team arrived on Friday, McMahon was as welcome in Boulder as a nuclear waste dump.

While being roundly booed he passed for 263 yards and three touchdowns in the opening half. He wasn't on target for eight hundred yards, but a five-hundred-yard day was within easy reach.

Then he did something to get on the crowd's good side. On the first series of the second half his left knee — his bad one — collapsed on an end-around, and he was carried off the field. As he passed in front of the cheering Colorado fans, he stopped worrying about his knee long enough to point an index finger at the scoreboard.

Steve Young, McMahon's backup, came in and kept everything level as BYU won 41-20. It was the Cougars' sixteenth win in a row, the longest winning streak in the nation.

But they were now without McMahon. During his absence they won one game, stretching the streak to seventeen with a 32-26 win over Utah State. But they lost the next week to Nevada-Las Vegas, 45-41. McMahon, meanwhile, was getting used to a thirty-pound knee brace fitted for his left leg so he could finish the season without having surgery. He had torn a ligament, but not to the extent that he absolutely couldn't use his leg. When his doctors asked McMahon what he wanted to do, he responded, "I want to make a run at the Heisman."

By game seven, against San Diego State and the Aztecs' new head coach, Doug Scovil, McMahon was making it. He completed twenty-seven of forty-two passes for 349 yards and three touchdowns in an intriguing matchup pitting the pupil against his mentor. The pregame question had been: Could the inventor stop his creation? The answer: Scovil felt like Dr. Frankenstein.

Then a curious thing happened. Working on a personal seventeen-game winning streak that dated back a year and a half, McMahon went to Wyoming—and lost. The Cowboys, a good team that would go 8-3 that season, not only had a particularly strong defense but they added a snowy field. McMahon was continually forced out of the pocket. He and his brace lost thirty-five yards rushing, and while he completed twenty-nine of forty-seven passes, it wasn't enough. By late in the fourth quarter Wyoming had an insurmountable 33-14 lead.

If there was one thing McMahon didn't know how to do, it was lose. He wouldn't allow Edwards to send in another quarterback. Taking over at the BYU twenty-yard line with 1:50 to play and a three-touchdown deficit, he ran onto the field, looked across the line of scrimmage at the Wyoming defense, raised his hand, and told them he was going to score a touchdown.

With seventeen seconds remaining he hit Dave Mills for a touchdown to end a length-of-the-field drive. As McMahon left the field the Wyoming defense gave him a standing ovation.

BYU could afford the Wyoming loss and still win the WAC, providing it could win the rest of its league games. New Mexico, Colorado State, Hawaii, and Utah stood in the way. The first three fell in order, which brought up the final, and most challenging, game—against the Utes in Provo.

Under coach Wayne Howard, Utah had enjoyed an excellent season. A defense anchored by tackle Steve Clark and linebacker Bill Gompf, and an offense that featured a strong offensive line and Del "Popcorn" Rodgers and Carl Monroe at running back, had lifted the team to an 8-1-1 record. In the WAC the Utes were 5-0-1. BYU was 9-2 overall and 6-1 in the WAC. The winner of this game would be the WAC champion, would get the Holiday Bowl berth, and, of major importance in one of college football's most intense instate rivalries, have all winter to gloat about it.

The largest crowd to ever assemble in the state of Utah gathered for the afternoon game. Cougar Stadium had thirty thousand seats. By adding additional chairs in the end zones and standing-room sections on the grassy areas in the north end zone, 47,163 fans crowded into the arena by kickoff. Another combined 9,512 were watching on closed-circuit television in BYU's Marriott Center and in the Special Events Center in Salt Lake City.

Part of Utah's enthusiasm was due to nearly a decade of frustration, and the prospect that it might end. BYU's comeuppance had been hardest on the Utes. For half a century the Cougars had been counted on to make Utah look good. BYU, after all, had won only six games in fifty years. But since 1972 the Cougars had won eight games in nine years. The tide had turned, and Utah was drowning. Here was a chance to turn it around.

Utah struck early. On the first play from scrimmage Rodgers went eighty-seven yards, north to south, for a touchdown.

McMahon and his brace took the field to answer. In the next five minutes he completed seven of eight passes and finished the eighty-four-yard drive with a touchdown pass to Scott Pettis. BYU never looked back, going on to win 56-28. McMahon completed thirty-five of fifty-four passes for 565 yards and four touchdowns. He was within six yards of Marc Wilson's NCAA record 571 passing yards—set against Utah in 1977—when they took him out.

It was one of the few records he didn't get.

McMahon ended the season with thirty touchdown passes and 3,555 passing yards in ten games—phenomenal until compared to what he'd done the year before. His career passing efficiency rating of 156.9 was an all-time NCAA high by more than four points. In total, he'd broken or tied seventy-one records in his career.

The Heisman Trophy eluded him, however. USC's Marcus Allen won the Heisman in 1981, and Georgia's Herschel Walker was second. McMahon was third. He reacted indignantly and blamed BYU, in part, for not promoting him enough.

In BYU's annual trip to the Holiday Bowl in San Diego—their fourth in a row—McMahon was faced once again with the task of trying to upstage what he'd already done. On the same field in the same bowl where he had last thrown the "Save the Game" pass to Clay Brown to win the 1980 Holiday Bowl over SMU, he started off by completing just one of six passes. Washington State, a school making its first bowl appearance in fifty-one years, had early false hope. After that McMahon settled down, passing for two quick touchdowns, one to Gordon Hudson and the other to his best friend Danny Plater—their last hookup to-gether—and by early in the third quarter BYU led 31-7. McMahon was en route to a 342-yard game, with thirty-seven completions in forty-three attempts, and the Offensive Player of the Game award. He was also not about to leave before doing something out of the ordinary.

Washington State mounted a second-half rally that pulled them within three points at 31-28. McMahon then engineered an eighty-two-yard drive that ended with an eleven-yard touchdown pass to Scott Pettis for a 38-28 lead. Then, when Washington State scored again and made the two-point PAT, to climb to within two at 38-36, it remained for McMahon to keep the football out of WSU's hands. It didn't matter if BYU scored again, the Cougars just didn't want to give back the ball.

Deep in their own territory, on the BYU twenty-nine-yard line, the Cougars were faced with a third-and-one situation with 2:37 to play. McMahon called for a running play to fullback Waymon Hamilton. "I wanted to let him get hit," said McMahon. But he fumbled the snap and the ball dropped to his left. A Washington State recovery would put them within field goal range.

McMahon, who, because of the brace on his left knee, hadn't run with the ball all night, took the weight off his left leg, hopped forward on his good right leg, picked up the ball as Washington State's Mike Walker dove for it, and hopped forward five yards for a first down that meant the clock could be killed and BYU could go out a winner.

That was that. He had started twenty-eight games as a BYU quarterback and won twenty-five. And he had rewritten the NCAA record book in the process.

McMahon had plans to take some classes winter semester after the Christmas (and Holiday Bowl) break. He only needed nineteen hours to graduate in communications. But his first time back on campus there was a message in the football office that the standards office wanted to see him. McMahon called Pratley. "They're finally going to throw the book at me," he said, "now that I don't have any more eligibility." McMahon never called to confirm his suspicions. To this day, he is on probation as far as the standards office is concerned.

The next anyone at BYU heard, McMahon was the third player selected in the 1982 NFL draft, by the Chicago Bears. He never did return to BYU, which was somehow poetic. Aside from teaming up to produce the best passing game in the history of college football, the two had little else in common.

STEVE YOUNG

"UP WHERE WE BELONG"
—Joe Cocker and Jennifer Warnes, 1982

*C*ontrary to what scientists and stadium architects will tell you, quarterbacks know that football fields are not flat. If their team is ahead, the field is downhill. If they're way ahead, it can look like a ski jump. But if they're behind, the field can resemble the Matterhorn, looking up.

Steve Young looked at the Jack Murphy Stadium field in San Diego and thought he needed pitons and a rope.

He wasn't standing where no man had ever stood before, and certainly where no BYU quarterback had ever stood. Indeed, it had become a kind of rite of passage for BYU quarterbacks to finish the season by coming to the Holiday Bowl in San Diego and doing Houdini impressions; to get themselves in ridiculous fixes and then go to work on the locks. On December 23, 1983, it was Steve Young's turn. There was 3:57 left to play—just one second less than the time that remained in the 1980 Holiday Bowl when Jim McMahon rallied the Cougars with twenty-one unanswered points and a 46-45 win over SMU — and Missouri held a 17-14 advantage. BYU had the ball on its own seven-yard line — ninety-three yards to go, straight up.

Not that Young hadn't seen worse. The past four years had been a crash course in survival training. In the first place, getting the quarterback job at Pass U. had been no easy thing; and then, after all the work, he had experienced a unique kind of buyer's remorse. What had he gotten himself into? He had an idea how it must have felt to take over for Babe Ruth in center field, to take over at center for the Celtics when Bill Russell retired, to succeed Johnny Unitas. He knew how those guys felt — whoever they were.

Unlike his predecessor, Jim McMahon, who looked with scorn on the record-breaking that had preceded him, and who had then rewritten the book by establishing seventy-one NCAA total offense and passing records, Young preferred a no-look approach. "I don't even want to know," he said.

How high were the expectations? There were times — as in every Saturday — when Young wished Cougar Stadium would blow up. In 1982, his first full year of starting, he threw up before, and during, every game. He was sure every person on earth had his eye on the BYU passing attack. He thought the nine hundred million Chinese *did* care. He *knew* the sixty-five thousand fans who showed up weekly in the newly expanded Cougar Stadium cared.

Sheide, Nielsen, Wilson, and McMahon created the monster. It was his job to keep it fed. It would be fine with Missouri if he didn't succeed. At the moment, as the Mizzou defense dug in to protect a goal line that was ninety-three yards behind them, that was particularly obvious.

GREENWICH, CONNECTICUT
1961-1979

LeGrande "Grit" Young had a policy his kids couldn't figure. If they had a job, he'd buy the gas. If they didn't have a job, they bought the gas.

But it was his car and his money, so that's the way it was. And if the Young kids knew one thing, it was this: As a nickname, "Grit" fit. Grit Young believed in hard work and results, and he passed these values down the line. The only thing he didn't pass on to his five children—Steve, Mike, Melissa, Tom, and Jim, in that order—was a "Utah" first name like his.

The family had started in Utah. Grit and Sherry Young met at BYU in the 1950s when Grit—the nickname went back to childhood—played both ways on the Cougar football team, as a fullback and linebacker. His senior year, 1959, he led the Cougars in rushing with a 5.1 average on eighty-three carries for 423 yards. The team went 3-7 that year, which was not atypical. Despite some feelers from the pros, Grit enrolled in law school at the University of Utah, subsequently graduated, and went to work for the Anaconda Corporation as a lawyer and labor negotiator in their Salt Lake City office.

The Youngs lived in the Cottonwood area of the Salt Lake Valley. Their first two boys, Steve and Mike, were eight and six when Anaconda offered Grit Young a promotion and a new office in Manhattan.

The Youngs left Utah in 1969 and bought a home in Greenwich, just across the Connecticut state line from New York City. They paid $70,000 for a split-level at 27 Split Timber Place on the south side of town. It seemed like a lot of money at the time — it was a lot of money at the time—but who was to know what inflation and demand would do to property values? In the next few years Greenwich would become the wealthiest city, based on per capita income, in the United States. By the 1980s the Youngs were sitting on a $350,000 home.

Greenwich became *the* fashionable New York commute. Donald Trump moved to Greenwich. Professional athletes Tom Seaver,

141

Dorothy Hamill, Craig Swan, and Bobby Valentine became res-idents. Ivan Lendl built an estate there. Paul Newman built a house on the town's outskirts. Diana Ross and George C. Scott and Victor Borge moved in, as did any number of chief executive officers of major corporations in New York City. The Manhattan skyscrapers were forty minutes away when the trains ran smoothly, which was how Grit went to work every day.

While his parents faced quite a culture shock, eight-year-old Steve found that adapting to life in Connecticut was no big deal. There were kids everywhere; and if he was the only Mormon, that was no big deal either. Just about everyone was an "only" some-thing. The only Buddhist. The only Ethiopian. The only Ar-menian. The only Seventh Day Adventist. Like New York City, Greenwich, Connecticut, was a melting pot. A devout Mormon whose "peculiarities" included no drinking or smoking, Steve found as he got older that he couldn't change his ways even if he wanted to. At parties his friends had his milk supply ordered ahead of time. They "just said no" for him.

Steve was avid in everything he did. When he collected stamps or coins, he did it with a fervor, winding up with the best collection in the neighborhood. At school he was a straight-A student. He was on the National Honor Society at Greenwich High School, where his grade point average, due to taking several college-level courses that gave him higher credit, came out at 4.2. He wasn't a natural scholar. He wasn't nuclear-physicist smart. But he always did his homework.

In high school Steve's typical day was 6:00 A.M., seminary in Scarsdale, New York, twenty miles away; school and sports practice from 8:00 A.M. to 5:30 P.M.; dinner at home; a work shift at Carvel's Ice Cream store (for gas money); homework; and lights out.

Steve was not pushed toward sports, or football in particular. He was encouraged to work hard at whatever he did, and he could choose what it was. Grit played catch with Steve whenever he wanted, which was often, but talked rarely of his own football days at BYU.

In the summers Steve mowed lawns in the north part of Greenwich, where the estates were. If he wanted to think he wasn't particularly affluent, this helped. "Mothers would call their children inside because the lawn boys were there," said Steve. "They didn't want us to sweat on them."

In Greenwich the sports atmosphere for kids was healthy but hardly overindulgent. The Yankees and Knickerbockers and Jets and Giants and Rangers and you name it were forty minutes away. Greenwich didn't dote on its youth stars. In Little League they gave a boy a T-shirt at the Greenwich Community Center and told him to play ball. It was a big change in atmosphere for Steve, whose first experience with Little League baseball had been in Salt Lake City, where they held a draft to determine ability.

He liked this better. He played in all the organized leagues. And when he wasn't doing that he was playing with Mike, his younger brother by exactly two years (they were both born on October 11, which also happens to be LaVell Edwards' birthday). Mike and Steve were best friends, but it took them sixteen years to get there. For the first fifteen they circled each other. Mike was taller and leaner, Steve bigger and older. As far as Mike was concerned, his big brother was no great joy to follow in the family batting order. Steve had a head start on Mike, and he kept it. He never even *let* him win at anything. "Steve was really an uptight kid," said Mike. "Everything mattered. He was the kind of kid who, if somebody teased him about liking a fat girl, wouldn't go to school for a week."

Mike's problem in the early days was that his uptight older brother also happened to be the best natural athlete in Greenwich, and probably the entire metropolitan area. He was big, strong, fast, and he had, well, grit. He liked to tackle sports on his own terms. He didn't just play all the time. He *practiced*. He worked on fundamentals. He unabashedly idolized Roger Staubach, a no-frills, work-ethic kind of guy. He wanted to make it on his own. After Grit coached him in Little League one season, Steve asked him not to coach his teams any more. He didn't want the other kids to think he was getting preferential treatment because his dad was the coach.

You'd naturally expect that the coaches at Greenwich High

couldn't wait for Young's class to arrive. Just the opposite was true. The kids Steve's age happened to be somewhat off-the-wall. His sophomore class was nicknamed "The Lousy Bunch." In their first football game on the junior-varsity level, Mike Ornato, the head coach at Greenwich, watched them play and asked the jayvee coaches if he could take the team into the locker room for a talk. "It was a real serious talk," remembered Ornato. "They had embarrassed themselves on the field, and I told them they had two miserable years ahead of them if they didn't think about it and get it together."

Steve took the talk to heart. He took everything to heart. As seniors "The Lousy Bunch" won the west division title and played in the Connecticut state championship game. Local newspapers gave Young a nickname of his own, "The Magician."

He rewrote most of the school's passing records, although he wasn't sure how. For one thing, Greenwich ran the wishbone offense. For another, he didn't like to pass. It started, his dislike for the forward pass, during a junior-varsity game with "The Lousy Bunch" when he threw eight interceptions. It had been raining and the ball kept slipping out of his hand as he was about to throw — a problem that got worse before it got better. His passes looked as though they'd been released from a shotgun. The fact that he was left-handed didn't make them look any prettier.

Ornato tried to help his grip, and his passing, by having the woodwork teacher make a block of wood shaped like a football, which he attached to the end of a universal machine and had Steve work on daily to develop his arm strength.

Whenever possible, Steve would go to his real strength — his legs. He was already running a 4.6 forty-yard dash in high school, which is fast, especially if you're white. When Ornato would send in a pass play, Steve had a tendency to exercise his option — they were running the wishbone, after all — and run. "I'm not going to embarrass myself if I don't have to," he would say. He carried the ball 165 times his senior year for almost two thousand yards.

He'd gotten the starting quarterback job as a junior, when the senior starter, Bill Barber, injured his shoulder. Ornato put Steve in as a test in a practice scrimmage against New Canaan High

School. On the first play, which was supposed to be a pass, Steve dropped back and, true to form, dropped the ball. But then he picked it back up and, unsure about what to do, let his instincts take over. He started to run. Seventy yards later he was in the end zone. At first Ornato thought it was because New Canaan had a bad defense. But on Monday he looked at the films and realized for the first time what he had on his hands.

Football was hardly what Steve Young ate, drank, and slept. He was also captain of the basketball and baseball teams; and, in truth, baseball was his first athletic love. He spoke French fluently, took advanced calculus and college history, was president of his seminary in Scarsdale, was the youth leader of the Yorktown LDS Stake, and held down a steady job at the ice cream shop. To top things off, one of his girlfriends was Christy Fichtner, who may have been the best-looking girl in the greater metropolitan area. She later became Miss Texas and Miss USA.

So he wasn't one-dimensional, or oppressed. Neither was he overlooked by college recruiters — particularly those from area schools, including those in the Ivy League, where entrance standards were high but not so high that a 4.2 GPA couldn't qualify. Yale and Harvard were interested. Cornell wanted him to become a brain surgeon and play on the football team.

In football recruiting the biggest rush came from the University of North Carolina, where coach Dick Crum was developing a top-twenty program. He wanted Young as his next option quarterback. Crum became a fixture in the Young home. He helped do the dishes, he read stories to the younger kids. He told Grit that Steve would step in as a freshman as the backup quarterback to a senior. Steve visited Chapel Hill and was impressed. Two factors kept him from going there. One, he didn't talk like they all did. Two, all the Mormon kids he knew in Connecticut and New York went to BYU and came back giving the school rave reviews.

Grit had gone there, too. Grit had also gone to B. Y. High, when that prep school was in existence. He didn't tell Steve to go to BYU, or anywhere else for that matter. You can imagine his advice. He told Steve to stand on his own two feet and make his own decision.

The problem was, BYU wasn't showing much interest. In 1975 LaVell Edwards sent a football to Steve. That was it. Ted Simmons, the president of the local LDS stake, called Edwards during Young's senior season to lobby in his behalf; and Steve's uncle, Bob Steed, who lived in Centerville, Utah, collected a packet of press clippings and sent them to Edwards' office. Steed talked frequently to Norm Chow, the Cougar coach in charge of recruiting, about his nephew. "You mean John Young," said Chow when they first met, using Young's seldom-used first name.

Not until late in December, well after football season was over, did Young get invited to make a visit to Provo. He stayed for three days. In his first meeting with Edwards he was told they might not have a scholarship available. When he met with him again at the end of his stay, Edwards had reviewed Young's films and clips and had found a scholarship. They could use him, but they weren't sure where. On letter-of-intent-signing day the Cougars signed Steve Young by mail. A couple of years later, when he had gained more notoriety and the media was making a great deal of his heritage — that he was a great-great-great grandson of Brigham Young, the school's founder — he would say, "Yeah, well, it didn't help me get a scholarship."

1980

Three months was all he could handle.

He had never been good at being away from home, anyway. As a Boy Scout he had missed all the overnight camps with a turned ankle or a headache that happened coincidentally to come along the day of the trip. Now he had a cross-country case of homesickness, accentuated by the fact that after going through the indignity of two-a-days in August, he had been treated like the invisible man. He was on the jayvee team, barely — backing up Gym Kimball and Mark Haugo. McMahon was the varsity starter, with Eric Krzmarzick his heir apparent. Overall, Young was BYU's eighth-string quarterback.

He had gotten his first clue about where he stood early in the season. The way a new player found out if he was going to dress for the home varsity games was if he opened his locker and a game jersey was in there. If a game jersey wasn't there, he wasn't dressing.

For the first home game of the 1980 season, against San Diego State, Young's locker didn't have a jersey. He showed up, distressed and distraught, at Bob Steed's house that night at 2:00 A.M. That same weekend the North Carolina starting quarterback was injured, and his backup, a freshman named Rod Elkins, had become the starter. Elkins was the quarterback North Carolina took after Young turned the Tar Heels down.

At a junior varsity game the next weekend at Snow College in Ephraim, Utah, Young was sent in at quarterback after Kimball and Haugo had their turns. The old instincts took over. He picked up the football and ran with it, highlighting the fourth quarter with a quarterback-keeper, two-point conversion that won the game for BYU by a point. Young thought that might get him on the traveling squad, or at least on the list to dress for home games. It didn't.

The toughest blow came at the end of the season when Edwards told Young they wanted to turn him into a defensive back.

When he went home to Greenwich for Christmas break, he was not in a good mood. Unlike the other kids who came home raving about BYU, he was comparing it to Siberia. "Even the girls are ugly," he said.

He told Grit he was going to quit.

Grit said that was fine, but where was he planning on living?

This father-son exchange took place in the kitchen on Split Timber Drive, and would become quite famous in newspaper accounts across the country. Actually, there is some confusion on the part of the parties involved as to just how the wording went. Mike Young, who was in the other room, remembers Steve saying first that "even the girls are ugly," and then saying, "I'm going to quit," after which Grit said, "Steve, you can quit, but you can't live here."

Grit, on the other hand, says that "Steve was very distraught, and I remember telling him we don't quit in this family. I gave him quite a long lecture on not quitting."

Steve's version is this: "Whatever he said, he said it for effect. He knew the influence he had on me."

At any rate, after the exchange with Grit, and after Christmas break was over, Steve Young returned to Provo—and started back-pedaling. Being a defensive back was better than being nothing at all. And it was certainly preferable to quitting.

For a time, he was in a kind of limbo. He was still officially a quarterback, but the defensive coaches were treating him as though he was a defensive back. He did his winter workouts half and half, sometimes working on defense, sometimes throwing passes and working on offense.

Meantime, there was a major development that, for Young, was encouraging. Doug Scovil left to become the head coach at San Diego State and was replaced by Ted Tollner. Scovil hadn't been impressed by Young's arm and didn't think he would make a good BYU quarterback. Krzmarzick, a 6'5", 185-pounder from Fallbrook, California, who could have been Gifford Nielsen and Marc Wilson's triplet, was Scovil's personal choice to replace McMahon. Haugo was another of his favorites. (Both, as it turned out, transferred after Scovil left—Krzmarzick to the University of Florida and Haugo with Scovil to San Diego State. Neither ended up playing as a major college quarterback.)

Tollner would have his own ideas. Young bided his time by working out harder than he ever had. By the time spring practice was ready to begin he was in the best shape of his life. In the forty-yard dash he was timed in 4.42—a clocking usually reserved for people who run track.

Ironically, running such a quick forty almost clinched the switch to free safety. Defensive coordinator Dick Felt was all for signing a defensive back with that kind of speed, and he kept the pressure on Edwards to make the switch.

But Tollner had been asked by Edwards to scrutinize all the quarterbacks and make his own conclusions. Unobserved, he walked into the Smith Fieldhouse annex one afternoon and watched them throw. He went directly to Edwards' office.

"Young throws it like a dart," said Tollner. "He doesn't have great velocity, but he has a tremendous release. And his foot speed is good."

"I think we've got a chance to have another great one," he said.

Edwards called Young into his office. He told him they would give him a two-week tryout at quarterback during the spring. Young said thank you and walked out. He was in the best shape of his life. He was sure two weeks would be plenty.

1981

Grit Young's work required him to travel. In the last week of September 1981 he got creative with his itinerary and arranged to return to New York by way of Boulder, Colorado. BYU was playing the University of Colorado that afternoon. Grit met his brother-in-law Bob Steed, who had flown to the game from Salt Lake City, and they found their seats high up in Folsom Field, where 43,259 fans had come to see what, if anything, the Buffs could do about Jim McMahon. The newspapers had printed McMahon's pregame comment, that he thought he could throw for eight hundred yards against the Colorado defense, and the mood in the stands was somewhere between indignation and lynch mob.

Since Chuck Fairbanks had taken over as coach two years earlier, Colorado's once-proud football tradition had hit on hard times. The Buffalos had won four games in two years while losing eighteen. The result was an ornery bunch of players, and even ornerier fans. No less than seven BYU starters would be hurt in the game. Bart Oates, the Cougars' starting center, went out early with an injury. So did Dan Plater, the Cougars' top wide receiver. The Colorado fans wanted more. The game was closer than normal for BYU. It wasn't the kind of day a backup quarterback could expect much playing time.

In the stands, Grit leaned over to Steed. "Too bad," he said. "I was hoping we'd get to see Steve today."

In BYU's first three games of 1981 Young had seen mop-up

duty every time. He'd completed eight passes in seventeen tries in wins over Long Beach State, Air Force, and UTEP, and had thrown his first-ever collegiate touchdown pass in the UTEP game.

Early in the third quarter the Colorado fans had their fondest hopes realized when McMahon went down and didn't get back up. He had severely hyperextended his knee and was carried off the field.

"I didn't want to see him this badly," said Grit.

Trotting onto the field with a clean blue number 8 on the middle of his white jersey was Steve Young. Just thirty seconds before he had been, by his own admission, "checking out the cheerleaders."

Just six months before he hadn't even been a quarterback. But Young had gone into his two-week trial at spring practice and passed at the top of his class. The more Tollner saw of him, the more he liked what he saw. They worked on improving his velocity and on his drop back; by the end of the spring he *looked* like a quarterback even if, at 6'2" and 198 pounds, he was built more like a fullback. He was officially third string, behind McMahon and Eric Krzmarzick, but no one, including Krzmarzick, believed that Young wouldn't be the first one in should McMahon need to be replaced.

Now, in the fourth game of the season, with the Cougars ranked eleventh in the country and riding a twelve-game winning streak, that was verified.

This wasn't how it had been for McMahon, who had paced like a prisoner before replacing Marc Wilson; nor was it how it had been for Wilson, who at least had a week of preparation when Gifford Nielsen blew his knee out in 1977—also in the fourth game—and had to be replaced.

Young looked at the Colorado defense and was sure they had twenty players on the field for defense, at least. He almost told the officials. He started to count them. He was in the early stages of shock.

Then he called a play in the huddle—Tollner had ordered a run, something easy on the new QB. He went to the line of scrimmage. Lloyd Eldredge, the starting right guard, yelled, "Get out of it, get out of it." Young hadn't looked at the defense too clearly. He assumed Eldredge had, and was telling him the running play wouldn't work and he'd better call an audible. His good friend, Gordon Hudson, was at tight end. "Red 65," Young said, indicating a pass to the tight end.

Young took the snap, dropped back, looked straight at Hudson, lost a solid grip on the ball, and released the pass. It flew ten yards over Hudson's head . . . directly into the hands of wide receiver Glen Kozlowski, who caught the ball in full stride for a twenty-six-yard gain. On the next play Young dropped back to pass, was forced out of the pocket, and scrambled for twenty-eight yards. He overthrew Plater in the end zone on the next play, and then hit Hudson with an eleven-yard touchdown pass.

When Young came off the field, Tollner was curious. Why had he audibilized out of the running play?

"Lloyd told me to get out of it," said Young. "So I threw it to Koz streaking down the side."

Then Young went over to Eldredge. "Why did you tell me to get out of that play?" he asked.

"I wasn't talking to you," said Eldredge. "I was talking to the line. We had to change how we were lining up."

Young improvised the rest of the day. Throwing and hoping, he looked like he'd been born to quarterback. He threw two touchdown passes and ran four times for sixty-one yards — a 15.25-per-play average. McMahon told reporters in the locker room he was worried for his job. Up in the stands, Grit Young had to leave as the game ended to catch a plane. No one knew who he was, which, under the circumstances, was probably a good thing. He was responsible for the latest quarterback phenom at BYU — the school with quarterbacks that wouldn't quit.

With amazing swiftness Steve Young was flung into the nation's media consciousness. Media consciousness is an odd thing. A lot of athletes and movie stars and singers and great artists can perform great feats yet languish forever in relative obscurity. Usually it's because they don't have a gimmick. Young, whether he liked it or not, had a gimmick. He was Brigham Young's great-great-great grandson. His great-great grandmother had been Emily Augusta

Young, who was named after her mother, Emily Dow Partridge, who had been one of Brigham Young's wives.

Steve Young wasn't Brigham Young's only relative. Marc Wilson had been distantly related, and no one had noticed. The Young family had given it little more than passing mention growing up. It didn't get them a tithing reduction.

It did get Steve Young attention.

"Brigham Young Would Have Been Proud of a Kin Named Steve," said the *Denver Post's* headline after he had beaten Colorado. By the next weekend both the *Deseret News* and *Salt Lake Tribune* traced his genealogy and published it for their readers. (It went like this: Brigham Young married Emily Dow Partridge and they had Emily Augusta Young, who married Hyrum Bradley Clawson and they had Carlie Louine Clawson, who married Seymour Bicknell Young and they had Scott Richmond Young, who married Louise Leonard and they had LeGrande Young, who married Sherry Ann Steed and they had John Steven Young.) In New York City, David Hartman of "Good Morning America" called and asked if Steve Young could be on the show.

Beyond the Brigham Young angle — there was romance there, no question, a direct descendant of the school's founder and namesake leading it to the modern promised land, namely, the top twenty — Steve Young had what the politicians call charisma. He was an All-America prototype. He had blue eyes, curly black hair, Hollywood good looks, and when he talked he came off as both confident and humble. (Later on, when Leigh Steinberg became his professional agent, Steinberg suggested that once they got the football out of the way they should think about Steve Young for President — of the United States.)

Young dressed casually, in Levi's and high-top basketball shoes with the laces undone, and drove around campus in a navy blue 1965 Oldsmobile that had more than two hundred thousand miles on the odometer. As the stories came off the presses, Young was pictured leaning on the hood of the car and was depicted as laidback and loose.

Just the opposite happened to be true. He was neither laidback nor loose. Otherwise, he certainly wouldn't be Jim Mc-

Mahon's understudy, or a quarterback at all. Nor would he be majoring in both business/finance and international relations, and carrying a 3.4 grade point average.

Two thousand miles away, he was still his father's son.

The car had been a gift from Grit—to Steve at first, and then to both Steve and Mike when Mike came to BYU. "It was a huge thing, for him to give us his car," said Steve. Grit Young had owned maybe four cars in twenty-five years. He treated them as though they were members of the family. He bought the Oldsmobile new when the family still lived in Utah. The family had driven to Park City when Steve was four and bought it at Bill Mawhinney Motors. It had been across the country in Connecticut all those years, and now it was back in Utah, still running strong. Grit had sent a three-page set of instructions with Steve, a personalized owner's manual. Whenever Steve knew Grit was coming to town, he'd change the oil.

Between studies and football, Young did little else. He went on few dates while at BYU. He had a hard time calling girls and starting out by saying, "Hi, this is Steve Young . . . " His close friends tended to be his teammates—Hudson at first, and then punter Lee Johnson and defensive end Jim Herrmann. By their senior year Johnson, Herrmann and Young were inseparable. They lived together in an apartment off campus, and Herrmann and Johnson—two guys who were loose and laid-back—kept life sane for Young, who was always under some kind of pressure, either from within or from without. It came with the calling.

No sooner had the pressure eased from the Colorado game than it picked up again. McMahon's knee was examined and he would be coming back with a brace, but not for two weeks. The nation's longest winning streak (sixteen games), a number-ten national ranking, and instate prestige against Utah State—a school McMahon had beaten 70-46 the year previous—were all in Young's hands.

He walked around campus hoping something would happen to the stadium. Something bad.

"I wanted it to blow up," he said. "I'd pray that it would blow up before Saturday."

He was sure what he had done at Colorado had been a fluke. He envisioned Sunday's headlines: "Young Chokes."

Game day came and he threw up—a ritual of his very own invention that would continue until he left BYU (as would the secret hope that the stadium would blow to smithereens).

Then he went out and completed twenty-one of forty passes for one touchdown and just one interception. He ran for his life again, gaining sixty-three yards on twenty-one carries. When the pocket would start to break down, Young would get out fast. It was just enough. The Cougars beat Utah State 32-26.

The winning streak was intact for another week. Details were set for Young's trip to New York to be on "Good Morning America"—immediately following the next week's game against Nevada-Las Vegas—and at practice Young stayed until they turned the sprinklers on. He never did leave practice early. He didn't like to practice, he loved to practice. Backup quarterback Blaine Fowler called him "a workaholic. He never wanted you to replace him, even in practice. He always wanted forty more balls."

McMahon was Young's mentor, although McMahon didn't always know it. Young didn't ask a lot of questions, but he watched and studied McMahon incessantly. They were roommates on the road, and they talked then; but mainly Young just watched and copied America's best quarterback. He dropped back like McMahon, he learned to throw like McMahon, he studied defenses the way McMahon studied defenses. "I don't ever remember him drawing up an X or O," said Young. "Jim just went by how it looked. He had a tremendous feel for how it was supposed to look." Young had always held McMahon in awe. When he was a freshman Young had given McMahon, then a fourth-year junior, a ride home. "I wondered what he did, where he went," said Young. Of course, so did a lot of people.

Young threw up before the UNLV homecoming game, too. He ran well that day—eighty-nine yards on twelve rushes—and completed the same percentage of passes that he had against Utah State—twenty-one of forty for one touchdown. But his old nemesis, interceptions, got in the way. He threw four. UNLV came back in the fourth quarter to win 45-41. If Young had been a free safety, he might have been able to stop the winning touchdown pass.

McMahon was back in time for the next game, at San Diego State. Young threw only four more passes the rest of the season, completing one, as McMahon ran out the string with five wins in six games and another conference championship. Young was content to watch and study. In the Holiday Bowl against Washington State he took a pitchout from McMahon and threw a twenty-six-yard completion to Hudson, setting up a McMahon-to-Plater touchdown pass on the next play. After the game — a 38-36 Cougar win — he returned to Greenwich for the holidays. A lot had happened in a year. McMahon was going to the NFL, and in three months Steve Young would start spring practice — as BYU's newest Air Apparent.

1982

It was early in the morning in Athens, Georgia, and without looking Steve Young knew what was going on outside. He had ears. It was raining. Not a heavy rain, not hurricane or tornado strength — which wouldn't have been so bad because they'd have cancelled the game — but light, mistlike, consistent rain. Young noticed it hitting the airplane window flying into Atlanta the night before. He hoped it would stop; he prayed it would stop. But it hadn't, and now he was lying in bed, listening.

He had a waking nightmare about rain, dating back to his sophomore year in high school and the eight interceptions in one game. The ball kept slipping out of his hands, and he kept throwing it away. In the 1982 opener the week before, played on a frying pan of a field in Las Vegas, where the field temperature had been 120 degrees just prior to kickoff, he completed nineteen of twenty-six passes and threw just one interception in a 27-0 win. ESPN had shown the game around the country. So far so good. Taking them a game at a time wasn't a cliche, it was a good idea. As for what McMahon had done, the seventy-one NCAA records and the 25-3 record as a starter, Young wouldn't even allow himself to think about it.

But the rain—that was another matter. You couldn't ignore the rain, not on a game day Saturday in Athens, Georgia.

The University of Georgia had won the national title two years before, and in Herschel Walker they had the best running back in the country. The Bulldogs had just lost a Monday night game against Clemson, the defending national champion, on network TV, so they weren't in a good mood.

BYU was still new at playing other nationally ranked programs during the regular season. Games with Pittsburgh, UCLA, Washington, Texas, and Baylor were set up for later seasons. But for now, Georgia ranked as the most formidable opponent BYU, in its sixty-year football history, had ever played. This was a school in the football belt, where they treated the sport like a religion. As the BYU bus drove to the stadium, there wasn't a marquee in town without a "Go Bulldogs" or "Hunker Down Dawgs" message. Young saw them through the windshield wipers on the way to the stadium.

Then, since he had no choice, he suited up and took the field. There was nothing else he could do.

Except throw five interceptions in the first half.

The high school nightmare was headed fast for second place.

The only good news was that Georgia wasn't doing any better. At halftime the score was 7-7. No one got alarmed. Edwards didn't say anything to Young except, "Come out throwing."

Being the visitor in such a setting doesn't make for an ideal situation, particularly when it's raining and you'd like to get a dry ball to throw. Bart Oates, the BYU center, kept asking the official for another ball. "I'm sorry, boy, but we don't just give you a new ball every play," said the referee.

But Young had calmed down. His natural instincts took over. He threw only one more interception in the second half, and the Cougars took a 14-7 lead going into the fourth quarter. Georgia had to mount a sixty-four-yard drive midway through the quarter to tie the game. The key play came when Georgia quarterback John Lastinger fumbled on fourth down at the BYU seventeen-yard line and Walker fell on the ball for a one-yard gain that kept the drive alive and set up the touchdown. The Cougars insisted they had gained control of the fumble; but when they uncovered the pile, Walker had the ball. Years later, when they were both in the NFL, Walker confessed to Young, "I gotta tell you. They bumped the ball to me, after the whistle." That call, and a last-minute Georgia field goal, was enough hunkering down to get the Bulldogs a bare 17-14 win.

The next weekend's game was in Provo, where it was dry and fair—ideal weather for the opening of the new Cougar Stadium, the house Sheide-Nielsen-Wilson-McMahon built. Remodeling had expanded the thirty-thousand-seat stadium to a sixty-five-thousand-seat structure with VIP loges, a plush president's loge, and an expanded press box. Somehow it fit that on top of everything else, Young had inherited a brand new stadium along with the accompanying mortgage.

Air Force was the opposition. Every new Cougar Stadium seat was filled. Young rushed for ninety-seven yards on twelve carries and three touchdowns, and he threw for 219 yards and one touchdown. It wasn't quite enough. Air Force won 39-38.

Brigham Young's great-great-great grandson was a not-so-great 2-3 in lifetime starts; and after the Air Force's wishbone had ruined the new stadium's inauguration party, people were starting to wonder. Young was new, Ted Tollner—who had gone to USC as the head coach—had been replaced by Mike Holmgren, a thirty-four-year-old quarterback coach from San Francisco State, and the good old days were fading fast.

"If this thing falls apart," Holmgren said to Young, "you know who they're going to point the finger at. I'm following Doug and Ted, you're following all the quarterbacks . . . "

Holmgren had sized the situation up quickly. He had coached the quarterbacks and been the offensive coordinator at San Francisco State. He had played quarterback at USC. He was the youngest quarterback coach at BYU since Dewey Warren.

A game against UTEP could not have come at a better time. In the past five seasons the Miners had fallen 68-19, 44-0, 31-7, 83-7, and 65-8 to BYU. If BYU needed a win, they could count on UTEP. In El Paso, Young rushed for ninety-seven yards and threw for 399 yards as the Cougars won 51-3. He'd saved his job for another week.

The 1982 BYU football team didn't have to regroup only at quarterback. A number of top receivers, including Danny Plater, had graduated with McMahon, and the offensive line was in a state of flux. The team struggled along with its new quarterback.

The Cougars lost to Utah State, 17-20, in their only other nonleague contest after UNLV and Georgia. They had closer-than-usual WAC games with Hawaii (39-25), Colorado State (34-18) and Wyoming (23-13). Only against San Diego State, in a 58-8 rout in Provo, did the Cougars go wild. Young had incentive playing against Doug Scovil, the coach who hadn't wanted him. He rushed for ninety-four yards and two touchdowns and passed for 284 yards and two more.

The Cougars were 7-3 after beating San Diego State and 6-1 in the WAC. The final game of the regular season was against Utah in Salt Lake City. To win the WAC and a Holiday Bowl berth the Cougars had to beat the Utes. New Mexico had already finished its season, at 6-1 in the WAC and 10-1 overall, and needed a BYU loss to make plans to spend the holidays in San Diego.

Utah was 3-3 in the WAC and 5-5 overall and not in the running for any postseason honors. There was a winning season on the line, however, and the added incentive that comes with playing your bitterest rival. The Utes, still upset about losing 56-28 the year before and getting knocked out of the Holiday Bowl, were at a fever pitch for the game. As the BYU bus came into the parking lot, Utah students rocked it back and forth. Security officers were summoned to escort the BYU players to their locker room.

After spending the year worrying, after constantly wishing damage to the new stadium in Provo, after assuming all the pressures of taking over as quarterback at BYU, Young really heaped it on himself for the Utah game. By BYU standards, he hadn't had a great year. He had thrown for more than three hundred yards just three times. He had never thrown more than two touchdowns in a game. He had a habit of running from trouble.

But this game against Utah could get him over the hump. If he could just win the WAC, he'd be all right. He told himself that he'd have done what Marc and Jim and all of the rest had done. He'd have won the league title and gone to a bowl. He wouldn't have to worry about comparisons anymore.

It was a cold day in late November, not an ideal day to pass the ball. Clouds hung low on the Wasatch Mountains, and it threatened to snow. Neither team's offense warmed up early. The defenses held well. Late in the first quarter Young passed to Mike Eddo for a 7-0 BYU lead. In the third quarter, after scrambling, Young hit Casey Tiumalu with a second touchdown pass to extend BYU's lead to 17-6. Young rushed only six times all day, his second lowest total of the year, and gained fifteen yards on the ground. But he threw his passes like darts, completing twenty-four of thirty-two with no interceptions. In a rugged, hard-nosed football game, BYU won 17-12; and as he walked off the field Steve Young felt a load float off his back.

"I remember that feeling, after we won," said Young. "It was the biggest win of my life. It started to snow right after the game ended. We drove home to Provo in the snow. We had beaten Utah for the conference championship. I never worried again about replacing anybody. I'd answered to myself. It was a big break-through. It led to everything else that happened."

Young went to his apartment in Provo that night, collapsed on the sofa, and watched "The Love Boat" on TV.

1983

The 1982 season hadn't ended happily ever after, however. The good news coming out of the regular season-ending win over Utah was that Steve Young had Found Himself and that BYU, by virtue of clinching its seventh straight WAC championship, would be off to San Diego for the Holiday Bowl again — for the fifth straight year.

The bad news was that Ohio State was the other team.

Meeting Ohio State in the bowl season of 1982 was a little

like meeting Joe Frazier just after he'd lost to Muhammad Ali. The Buckeyes would have been playing up the road in Los Angeles, in the Rose Bowl, except for an uncharacteristic slow start to the season. They were arguably the nation's best football team by season's end. They lost three early games, to Stanford, Florida State, and Wisconsin. Then they had been unbeatable. In the last game of the regular season they had beaten Michigan, the team that was playing in the Rose Bowl. In San Diego, the Buckeyes were not in a good mood. Earle Bruce, the Buckeye coach, approached the game as though it was the landing of Normandy. He chased the Utah media from his practices, afraid they might be spies, and stationed his weight-training coach at the entrance to the Buckeyes' practice field to screen all visitors.

The Buckeyes had red meat for their pregame meal and went out on the evening of December 17 and blew away the Cougars, 47-17. Except for a 49-17 loss to Arizona State in 1972, it was the worst loss ever for a LaVell Edwards-coached team. Running back Tim Spencer rushed for 167 yards, including a sixty-one-yard touchdown run in the second quarter that erased an early BYU lead. The score was 34-10 after three quarters, when the bulk of the 52,533 in attendance started to leave. The situation was similar to two years before, when SMU had led by three touchdowns at the end of three quarters and the stands began to empty. But on this night, there was to be no miracle finish.

Young had a decent game statistically, throwing for 341 yards with twenty-seven completions on forty-five attempts. But three times the Cougars turned the ball over inside the thirty-yard line. The Buckeyes went back to Columbus convinced they were the best team in the land.

They had Young's vote. They had opened his eyes and in an ironical sort of way served as an inspiration for the BYU team coming into the 1983 season. "I don't think there was anyone who played in that game who wasn't impressed by the level Ohio State was playing on," said Young. "It helped, knowing how much better our game had to be to get to that level. All off-season it helped."

For Steve Young, there was still the fear factor, too — the fear of being the first quarterback to steer the ship onto a rock. It's amazing the motivation that can come from self-preservation. Young was driven to whip himself into even better shape as he prepared for the 1983 season, and so was Holmgren, the quarterback coach who was feeling the pressure himself. And so, too, was Norm Chow, the receivers' coach who had been elevated upon Tollner's departure for USC to call the plays from the press box. Holmgren and Chow were splitting the duties formerly held by one coach—from Dewey Warren to Dwain Painter to Wally English to Doug Scovil to Ted Tollner. Holmgren was the quarterback expert and Chow, who shared an office with Scovil for years and had, in the process, become familiar with the BYU offensive concepts, called the plays. If Holmgren wanted to call a play during the course of a game, he could do that, too, and it was his responsibility to prime the quarterbacks in the fine art of audibilizing at the line of scrimmage. McMahon had audibilized as much as 50 percent of the time.

Young and Holmgren grew as close as you might expect for two men in the same foxhole.

They could yell at each other and forget about it by the snap of the next ball. That kind of close. As is the case with most perfectionists, Young tended to be strong-minded. Holmgren could handle that. He acted as a mediator between Young and Roger French, who was the offensive coordinator as well as the offensive line coach and whose personality clashed with Young's.

In 1982, Young's tendency had been to run away from trouble. If a play even started to look shaky, he would tuck the ball under his arm as though he was a mail carrier starting on his rounds and look for daylight. It was a natural reaction for someone with his speed—a "you'll-have-to-catch-me-first" approach to danger. But it was getting away from Doug Scovil's bible, the playbook the Cougars continued to use.

Holmgren explained this to Young daily. Stay in the pocket just a little longer. Look for the third receiver, then the fourth. Check them off. Study the old films of Sheide, who may have done it better than anyone. Study the win-loss records of pocket-stayers Sheide-Nielsen-Wilson-McMahon—a cheap shot, there, bringing up the old ghosts who had made all of this necessary. But the point was clear: They had all thrived under the system of pass-first-run-later. And the truth was, with a starting record of 9-5 heading into his senior year, Steve Young wasn't in their league.

After one game into the 1983 season, he was 9-6.

The Cougars traveled to Waco, Texas, to open against the Baylor Bears, and when the dust had cleared and was floating over the Brazos River the Bears had a 40-36 win. It had been their good fortune to have the ball last. Another couple of minutes and BYU would have gone ahead, no doubt. It was that kind of game. Back and forth with no discernible defense. Young was as hot as he'd ever been, completing twenty-three of thirty-eight passes for 351 yards and rushing thirteen times for 113 yards, his career high. His 464 yards individual total offense would be the third highest of his career, and he did not throw an interception.

Still, the Cougars lost, and in their opener, which is never pleasant. But as the plane headed back for Provo, Young had a strange feeling—for him, a pessimist at heart, a very strange feeling. He thought this team that was 0-1 and unranked was headed in the right direction.

The next week he threw five touchdown passes in Cougar Stadium against Bowling Green in a 63-28 win.

Young threw three more touchdown passes in a 46-28 win against a good Air Force team the next week. The craziness was returning. The Cougars had given up fifty-six points in the last two games. They had scored 109.

Then came a game against UCLA in Los Angeles. Another in the line of big-time games BYU was lining up now that it had a sixty-five-thousand-seat stadium to bargain with. UCLA had been more than happy to agree to a home-and-home with the Cougars, with one stipulation: the first game would be in Pasadena in the Rose Bowl.

As only Californians can do, and, in particular, Californians who live on the freeways in Los Angeles, the UCLA fans made it clear from the start that BYU should feel lucky just to be there, smelling the roses. Only half of the one-hundred-thousand-seat stadium was filled. As Young came through the tunnel and onto the field for warm-ups, one of the fans shouted, "What is this, high school night?"

BYU played like it had been in the Rose Bowl every week. The final score was BYU 37, UCLA 35, but the Cougars never trailed and led comfortably throughout the game. UCLA's final score came with just twenty-six seconds remaining. As they left the field the Cougars celebrated as if they had won the Rose Bowl— instead of merely playing in it. Edwards rated it as "one of the great wins we've ever had."

Young had personally had one of the worst days of his career. He threw for just 270 yards. And while he completed two passes for touchdowns, he also threw three interceptions.

It was a much inferior performance to what he had done three weeks earlier at Baylor. But the Baylor game was a loss and this game was a win, for one thing; and for another, it was a win played in a Media Capital.

It doesn't matter what you do as much as it matters where you do it.

The team flew back to Provo, but Young didn't. The great-great-great grandson of Brigham Young stayed over a day and appeared on the CNN "Sports Sunday" show.

To this point in the season, Steve Young's name and the term *Heisman Trophy* had not been mentioned in the same paragraph. By Heisman Trophy and BYU standards, he had had only a so-so year in 1982. In the preseason Heisman rankings Young was virtually ignored. The top five candidates were Nebraska running back Mike Rozier, Oklahoma running back Marcus Dupree, Duke quarterback Ben Bennett, Nebraska quarterback Turner Gill, and Maryland quarterback Boomer Esiason.

But then came the day in L. A., and suddenly Young was a contender. He was leading the nation in total offense, passing yardage, and passing efficiency; his team was 3-1 and finally ranked—the Cougars made it to number twenty after the UCLA win—and, most persuasive of all, he looked good on camera.

Wherever Young went after the UCLA game, microphones and notepads followed.

Wyoming fell 41-10, New Mexico 66-21. The Lobos tried a novel approach, similar to the one San Diego State had tried in its 63-14 loss to Marc Wilson in 1979. They rushed everybody. Young wanted to send them a thank-you card. He threw four touchdowns before leaving just after halftime. BYU wound up with 777 yards total offense.

Then San Diego State fell 47-12. Young couldn't help it. He got great satisfaction drilling Doug Scovil's team. He had the most passing yards of his career, 446, against the Aztecs. Utah State was the next victim, 38-34, as Young added to his resume by coming back from a concussion to nail down the win.

Sports Illustrated sent a writer and photographer for a major feature story on Young and Gordon Hudson, who was rewriting the NCAA record for tight ends. The article, headlined "The Steve and Gordon Show," appeared after UTEP fell 31-9 to run BYU's record to 8-1. Gil Brandt, the player personnel director for the Dallas Cowboys, was quoted as saying Young was the best BYU had ever had. "He's the most accurate passer I've ever seen. Period," said Brandt—a statement that would be proven prophetic when, at the end of the season, Young's 71.3 percent completion ratio established an NCAA record.

About this time Grit Young wrote Steve's brother, Mike, who was in Honduras on a mission. Mike had taken a leave of absence from the BYU football team after his freshman year in 1982. Grit told Mike, who was about to return home from his two-year mission, that he'd better brace himself. If for some reason they hadn't written it up yet in the Honduras sports sections, his brother, Steve, was turning into a household name, and not just in their household.

The day Mike got home the first program he saw on television was an in-depth feature ESPN did on his brother.

Not that any of it had much effect on Steve. Maybe *Sports Illustrated* was depicting him as "a well-muscled 198 pounds with curly black hair, a way with women and a certain Eastern swagger," and maybe they had pictured his 1965 Olds as the perfect student kick-around car, and maybe NFL experts were calling him the next Staubach. But Young was going about business as usual. He was almost ready to graduate — in his dual major — after just seven semesters. He was still steering clear of the social scene. (He could solve New Mexico's rush, but couldn't come up with a good opener on the telephone that didn't sound as though he was showing off.) At practice he was still asking for forty more balls and fidgeting nervously whenever his backup, Robbie Bosco, spelled him.

And he was still throwing up before every game.

It was the Friday night offensive team meetings that got to him. Holmgren and Chow would go over the next day's goals, which were getting ridiculous: four hundred yards passing, 70 percent accuracy, no interceptions, forty points, and a win. Did we miss anything? It was more effective than ipecac syrup. Young would go home and throw up.

But you'd never have known. It always looked so easy on Saturday. By the time the Utah game came along to end the regular season, the Cougars were ranked number nine in the country and were riding a nine-game winning streak. They had not lost since they ran out of time at Baylor.

The Utes were making their first appearance in the new Cougar Stadium, and it was as though they weren't there. BYU won 55-7. Young had saved his best for last. He threw six touchdown passes, the most of his career, and was otherwise close to perfect, completing twenty-two of twenty-five passes in limited playing time with no interceptions. The fact that he gained a minus-five yards rushing, on just five carries, verified that he had become a pocket-staying quarterback, just like The Other Guys.

After losing the opener to Baylor, the Cougars had won ten straight games and were ranked in the top ten. They led the nation in passing with 381.2 yards per game, and were even ranked in the top fifteen in rushing offense. They led the nation in total offense with 584.2 yards per game — an NCAA record that demolished the old mark of 566.5 set by Oklahoma in 1971 — and were number two in scoring with forty-four points per game. Any other year in history that would have easily been first, but 1983 was the year Nebraska went slightly berserk and averaged fifty-two points every game.

Young passed for 3,902 yards with thirty-three touchdown

passes and only ten interceptions. He completed 71.3 percent of his passes and had a passing efficiency rating of 168.3. He led the nation in all these categories, and a few others, including his total offense average of 395.1 yards per game; set thirteen NCAA records; and was named first-team quarterback on all the All-American teams. Despite a slow start, he finished second in the Heisman race to Nebraska's Rozier, who had rushed for more than two thousand yards and who played for the number-one-ranked (at the time) Cornhuskers. That had been an unbeatable combination. Even an intensive grass roots lobbying effort from BYU fans didn't turn the tide. Thousands signed their names to an eight-foot-high postcard and sent it to CBS sportscaster Brent Musburger, who showed it on the air.

Young's 168.3 efficiency ranking was the third highest ever—behind only McMahon in 1980 (176.9) and Tulsa's Jerry Rhome (172.6 in 1966). His career efficiency rating of 149.8 was second highest. Only McMahon's 156.9 was better.

BYU was the WAC champion, again, and would play in the Holiday Bowl, again. During the layoff before the December 23 game in San Diego, Steve Young did something he swore he'd never do. He peeked at what McMahon had done.

HOLIDAY BOWL VI

But if all's well that end's well, it was all unraveling now on a cloudy evening in San Diego when both the temperature and the ninth-ranked Cougars were fading fast. With a 7-4 record, Missouri had come into the game unranked and unexpected to make it a game. They had a quarterback, Marlon Adler, who spent his time in the film room studying Young, unabashedly hoping to copy him.

Then the game began and Missouri went ahead 7-0, then 10-7, and finally, on Eric Drain's second touchdown run early in the fourth quarter, the Tigers were up 17-14. Drain hadn't rushed for over one hundred yards all season but was en route to 115 yards on twenty-seven carries against BYU. Missouri was playing its best football of the season.

On BYU's next possession Young, who was having uncommon trouble (he had already thrown three interceptions), completed three of four passes; but the Cougars turned the ball over with a fumble. The Tigers took off on a five-minute drive that got them to the BYU seven-yard line on fourth down. Needing one yard for a first down, they gave the ball to Drain, who went straight up the middle and leaped in the air — only to find a surprise. He met the entire BYU defense, some of them for the first time, and was stopped for no gain.

Now BYU had the ball with 3:57 on the clock and ninety-three uphill yards to cover.

As he came out to the field for what he believed would be his last series as a Cougar quarterback, it was as it had always been for Steve Young: not exactly easy. Because of numerous demands on his time, Young's bowl preparation had been inconsistent. Being the nation's consensus All-American quarterback had carried with it certain obligations. He'd gone to Dallas to be awarded a top-five, scholar-athlete award from the NCAA. He'd been a regular on "Good Morning America" — setting what was believed to be a college quarterback record with three consecutive weekly appearances. As a member of the Associated Press All-America team, he did the "Bob Hope Christmas Special" on television. Amid it all, Holmgren had even gone to the BYU sports publicity office and said sarcastically, "Do you think Steve can come to practice one day?"

Now Young was on the field with a do-or-die drive on his hands. His first pass went to Mike Eddo for seventeen yards. So far so good. His second pass, or at least his second pass attempt, never materialized. He was sacked for a loss of thirteen yards. On second-and-twenty-three he was nearly sacked again. But on the way down he saw Eddo wide open upfield. He quickly released a pass that Eddo stopped and waited for and then took for a fifty-three-yard gain. Two more completions produced another first down at the Missouri twenty-five yard line.

Then, in quick order, Casey Tiumalu was stacked up for a two-yard loss, Young threw an eleven-yard completion to Tiumalu, and Young was sacked for a nine-yard loss. The Cougars were back where they started, at the Missouri twenty-five-yard line, facing a fourth-and-ten. Less than a minute remained. Lee Johnson could easily nail a thirty-two-yard field goal for the tie.

But BYU didn't even call timeout. Perhaps Edwards was thinking back to the moment in the 1980 Holiday Bowl when McMahon insisted on turning fourth down into the start of a miracle. He sent in a passing play. Young dropped back, saw that Gordon Hudson and Kirk Pendleton were covered, and went to his third option, running back Waymon Hamilton, who was racing down the sideline. Hamilton reached out and brought in the pass, stayed inbounds, and stepped forward. He made the first down by a foot.

Twenty-three seconds remained, as did the 51,480 in attendance. The Cougars were on the fourteen-yard line. In the press box Chow sent word to Holmgren on the sidelines: "Call Fake Right 28, QB Screen Left."

Holmgren repeated the play to Eddie Stinnett, a black running back from Springfield, Ohio, who ran to the offensive huddle and repeated it to Young.

Young did a double take. Stinnett had a tendency to talk jive—"I never was quite sure what he said," said Young—and he wasn't sure he'd heard him right this time. "Fake Right 28, QB Screen Left" was not a garden-variety BYU play. As a matter of fact, it had never been called before. Besides that, Stinnett had turned the title into "Fake Sweep Right, Throw Back to the QB."

"Eddie, what did you say?" asked Young.

Eddie said, "Yeah, the QB pass."

They'd practiced the play sparingly. It belonged to the flea-flicker family. Seven such gimmick plays had been drawn up for the bowl game—plays that could be used once and thrown away.

Chow noticed that Missouri, in its man coverage, wasn't covering Young. He thought he'd make an excellent receiver.

In the press box, Chow watched with delight as Young stood up over the center and shouted out his count. The Missouri free safety had come up to the line of scrimmage. The trap was set.

Young took the snap and handed the ball to Stinnett, who pretended to sweep right and then stopped to loft a pass back to Young, who was now in the flat.

"I couldn't see Eddie," said Young. "I thought it wouldn't work. Then all of a sudden the ball comes flying to me."

A Missouri defender, Taft Sales, had a shot at the ball, but his leap missed by inches. The rest was easy. Young took in the ball, tucked it away, and slid across the goal line like it was home plate.

After catching the first pass of his college career, Young did something else he'd never done before. He celebrated the touchdown. When he saw the films later he wasn't sure it was him. He ran around in circles and performed a variety of newly invented dance steps. He looked like a schoolboy on the first day of summer vacation. A lot of people might have thought that Brigham's great-great-great-grandson was doing a little showboating. But they couldn't know where he was coming from.

ROBBIE BOSCO

*R*obbie Bosco's left knee was lying at an awkward angle on the training room table deep inside San Diego's Jack Murphy Stadium. It was the last place Bosco wanted to be, but he hadn't had much choice a few minutes earlier when he couldn't walk and they'd carried him there. Outside, a football game was going on—Brigham Young versus Michigan in the 1984 Holiday Bowl. When the game was only nine minutes old, with no score, Mike Hammerstein, a defensive tackle for the Michigan Wolverines, had introduced his 239 pounds to Bosco's left leg.

Hammerstein had gotten to both the knee and the ankle. He used a surprise attack, making his tackle well after Bosco had thrown and completed a pass to wide receiver Glen Kozlowski. Hammerstein was flagged for a late hit, but BYU was called for an illegal shift on the same play so the penalties offset each other and the play was declared void. Only try telling that to Bosco's knee, which, at the moment, was getting the kind of attention usually reserved for medical

170

school operations. Interested observers were everywhere. Doctors and trainers were probing the knee from all angles, trying to quickly determine the extent of the damage. There were still more than three quarters of football to be played and a Holiday Bowl score to settle. Beyond that, there was this matter of a national championship.

It hadn't figured, of course, to come to this. If Steve Young felt the weight of the world on his shoulders when he took over the BYU quarterback job from Jim McMahon, imagine what was running through Robbie Bosco's mind when they tossed him the ball. Young's Cougars had finished the 1983 season with an eleven-game winning streak. They had won the WAC and the Holiday Bowl, and been ranked number seven in the final AP and UPI polls. There were a lot of directions for Bosco to go, but not that many were up.

So he had come up with this, uh, gimmick. Hey, how about a national championship? Has anybody done that?

It had been a season of one good break after another. Murphy's law in reverse: Everything that could go right had gone right. The Cougars had done their part, winning every Saturday, and every other team in the country had obliged them by finding a way to lose — at least once. Every poll — USA Today, CNN, ESPN, and of course the big two, AP and UPI — had ranked the BYU Cougars, if you could believe it, number one in America at the conclusion of the regular season. If BYU could only win their annual bowl game in San Diego, who could argue with 13 and 0?

Michigan, a good team that had gone bad, had come to the Holiday Bowl in a kind of penitent mood. This was a 6-5 team that began the season ranked number four and expected by now to be 11-0 and playing in the Rose Bowl. Their coach, Bo Schembechler, an unpleasant man even when he was 11-0,

171

and a coach who had never won a national championship, snarled whenever he spoke—which wasn't often. The Wolverines didn't like their secondary role in this drama. They intended to do their talking on the field and show BYU how they play football in the Big 10. All of that was illustrated by Hammerstein's exuberance nine minutes into the game.

Bosco, on his back, waited for Dr. Brent Pratley, the team orthopedic surgeon, to complete his examination. Pratley, a flamboyant type who arrived at the game by driving his Rolls Royce from Provo to San Diego in record time, was working on another speed run. He checked the ligaments and tendons.

"So, what?" asked Bosco.

"The ankle will be all right," Pratley said. "If we brace the knee, the worst you've possibly got is a medial collateral ligament tear, and we can fix that. The chance of tearing the anterior cruciate ligament is like another lucky hit down the smokestack."

"I understand that," said Bosco. "Let's play."

They carried him back out.

ROSEVILLE, CALIFORNIA
1963-1980

Terry Bradshaw and Robbie Bosco were having breakfast in the coffee shop of the Houston Marriott, although not together. But as they would both be performing later that afternoon in the Astrodome, Robbie, who was thirteen, thought it would be all right if he went over to the table where the Pittsburgh Steelers' quarterback was sitting and ask him for his autograph.

This wasn't a bad deal at all, living on the road. He was missing school, dining with the rich and famous, and that afternoon he would be a contestant in the AFC Division finals of the National Football League's Punt, Pass and Kick contest. Robbie's hobby was Punt, Pass and Kick. He had survived the city finals in his hometown of Roseville, California, the area finals in nearby Yuba City, and the sectional finals in Oakland—held during half-time of a Raiders' game—to make it to Houston. Some kids collected stamps, or raised hamsters, or built model airplanes. Robbie had picked up a football when he was seven and hadn't put it down.

Not that punting, passing, and kicking was an obsession with him. To have an obsession you have to be driven, and if the youngest child of Louis and Elva Bosco was anything, he wasn't driven. Here was a kid any Californian could be proud of—laid-back, comfortable, an early believer that nowhere was so close that you wouldn't drive to it. Growing up, his most frequently spoken words were, "John's closer." As in, "Robbie, take out the garbage." To which Robbie would say, "John's closer."

John, Robbie's older brother by three years, would then say, "Robbie's closer." And Elva Bosco would take out the garbage.

How laid-back was Robbie? So laid-back that it led to an addiction when he was barely a teenager. He got hooked on the soaps. "General Hospital," in particular. He didn't miss an episode for years, and this was before videotape.

But when the mood would hit, he would take his football and go out and kick it. Or pass it. Or punt it. He would do it with John, or drag Elva to the park, or throw to Lou in the backyard. Often he would do it alone. It was something you could do alone, if you didn't mind shagging your own football. He broke three windows in the neighbor's house, and put out the window in the family car one afternoon; but it had paid off, hadn't it? Here he was in Houston, just one good pass, punt, and kick away from going to the national finals, to be held at the Super Bowl.

Of the three disciplines, he preferred passing. You couldn't shank a pass. But he was about equidistant with all three. At thirteen he could punt, pass, and kick a football an average of forty yards each.

At the Astrodome finals he wasn't off form, but he didn't hit career marks, either, and he wound up second. He put his Super Bowl plans on hold and returned home to his seventh-grade routine. A lot of the kids didn't even know where he'd been, or that

173

he had developed this knack of flinging and kicking a football uncommonly long distances.

Chiefly this was because, through age thirteen, Robbie had never played any kind of team football. He hadn't played real tackle football, as in the Pop Warner or Ron Chapman Little League programs that thrived in Roseville. Many of his friends played Little League football and had done so since they were eight, but Robbie hadn't joined them. He liked football as a noncontact sport.

If he wanted contact, there was always John. Despite the three-year age differential, the brothers were always together, and always playing one sport or another. They got away with a lot at home because of the slack taken up by their two older sisters, Loretta and Cindy, who *would* take out the garbage.

Lou and Elva Bosco moved to Roseville in 1956, seven years before Robbie, their youngest, was born. They bought a three-bedroom rambler on Evelyn Avenue and went about the process of being California-ized. Both Lou and Elva were born and raised in Price, Utah, amid the coal mines. Lou had been named the outstanding athlete at Carbon College in Price (class of 1949) where he played football, basketball, and baseball. But he'd left sports and Price behind and gone to Utah State University in Logan for his bachelor's degree in education. When the Roseville School District offered him a teaching job at the junior high school, he and Elva moved to Roseville.

Roseville was a city of thirty-five thousand people located nineteen miles southwest of Sacramento, just above the California Delta. San Francisco is one hundred miles to the southwest, Reno and Lake Tahoe are two hours in the other direction. The city was first established as a railroad town on the Southern Pacific line. In the 1970s high tech industries moved in. The crime rate was low, befitting a town within an easy drive of three of America's most notorious prisons — Vacaville, Folsom, and San Quentin. A fourth, Alcatraz, shut down when Robbie was just starting to punt, pass, and kick. Another Roseville distinction is that the San Francisco 49ers hold their summer training camp there.

The Boscos grew up more or less like Ozzie and Harriett. The

174

family stayed at home a lot and did things such as play board games, although Robbie did have a hobby that kept him out nights. He liked the movies. He'd meet his buddy, Darren Woessner, at the Tower Theatre for double features. Afterward, they would walk to the corner, by Bud's Cleaners, at which point each would be about a dark quarter of a mile from home. They'd take off on a dead sprint, and then call each other to make sure they'd made it home. Particularly after a horror film.

If it had been up to Robbie Bosco, macho would have never made it big. Not only didn't he play tackle football, and not only did movies scare him to the point that he'd sleep with the light on, but he preferred to be called Robbie. Even when he got older, he didn't want anyone calling him Robert—his full name.

Neither was he a social animal. As a teenager, when he needed a date to some school function, he would talk Woessner into calling a girl and saying it was him.

Robbie spent a lot of time in Roseville with a young neighbor friend, Tommy Owens, who had been born with a cleft palate and without an ear. He took Tommy to many of his games and, in general, doted on him.

Robbie didn't stay away from all team sports. He played on baseball and basketball teams when he was younger, although he had a bad habit of not getting around to signing up for baseball until the deadline had expired. When the season began he would invariably complain. Then the next year he'd miss the deadline again.

Lou and Elva Bosco weren't the driving kind, either. If Robbie couldn't get to the sign-ups on time, that was his problem. Lou Bosco did teach both John and Robbie the fundamentals of sports, whenever they felt inclined, and he was always their number-one fan. He just didn't care how far they took things. When he took Robbie to his first league baseball workout, he told him to hustle out to right field and keep out of the way. When Lou returned to pick him up two hours later, Robbie was pitching.

Robbie had two things going for him in sports. One was John, who blazed all the trails. And two, he was something of a natural. When Robbie was a freshman in high school, his football coach

175

watched him for exactly one afternoon and predicted a college scholarship was in his future.

Not that Robbie cared.

He had gone out for the freshman football team mainly because of peer pressure. He soon figured out how to put on the pads, and discovered that even the tackling and blocking wasn't all that bad. But after two weeks of workouts, he'd had enough just the same. And he quit.

John, a senior at Roseville High and the starting quarterback for the varsity, was the first to hear the news. He had encouraged Robbie to give organized football a try, because, of all Robbie's backers, John *knew* he could be a good one.

"You're quitting. Why?" asked John.

"Because I can't understand the plays," said Robbie.

He felt that a quarterback should have a good working knowledge of what was going on out there, and so far he didn't have a clue.

They spent two hours that night going over play-calling. John explained that even-numbered plays went to the right, odd-numbered plays to the left, and that the running backs were numbered — one, two, and three. Those were the basics. Decide which way you were going to run the play, and which running back was going to run it, and that was it, you had it down. It was certainly easier than geometry.

In a lobbying effort, several teammates — now former teammates — came over to Robbie's house; and after a couple of days Robbie said okay, he'd end his holdout, and he asked the coach if he could be reinstated.

He learned about contact soon enough. Roseville played a wishbone offense. Robbie would have preferred to pass or punt or kick, but he had deceptively good speed as well as a deceptively good ability to take the pounding that comes with getting hit on virtually every play (which is the quarterback's lot in the wishbone). You wouldn't know it by looking at him. He didn't touch a weight until his senior year of high school, and his idea of a good workout was a double feature. He used to haul his 6'3", 175-

pound body home from football practice, slump on the couch, and ask, "Does *this* look like the body of a wishbone quarterback?"

But he endured. And so did Roseville High. By his junior year the Tigers—who had always been a kind of perennial football weakling in the area—went 8-2 and played in the AA play-offs for the first time in years. In Robbie's senior season, in 1980, the Tigers had another winning season, at 6-4. In two seasons Bosco passed for over three thousand yards—amazing considering Roseville ran the wishbone—and was named not only MVP of the team but of the entire Sierra Foothill League.

He was also the MVP of the basketball and golf teams. On the golf course he consistently shot in the high seventies, but it was in high school basketball that he particularly shined. Following in the footsteps of John, who set a Roseville High single-game scoring record with fifty-one points and accepted a scholarship to play at a nearby junior college, Robbie played on the 1980 Roseville High basketball team that won the northern California championships, beating Anderson High School 76-72 in the title game played in the Oakland Coliseum.

Robbie would have loved to play college basketball, and was encouraged by a certificate signed by Frank Arnold, then head basketball coach at BYU, upon completion of the Cougar basketball camp during the summer before Robbie's senior year. The certificate read, "Robbie has great potential as a basketball player."

After Robbie attended that camp, Lou and Elva drove from Price, where they were visiting relatives, to pick him up in Provo and return to California. Wandering around the BYU campus they found themselves early one evening in the football stadium. Either Lou or Elva, they can't remember which, said, "How would you like to play in front of this many people?" To which Robbie said, "I can't even imagine."

But reality set in soon enough. College football recruiters came around after he threw for 1,823 yards as a senior, with fourteen touchdown passes and a 53 percent completion rate. The University of California-Berkeley, a team that threw the ball and was only an hour and a half away, came on strong. So did the Oregon schools. San Diego State, with new head coach Doug Scovil, offered Robbie a full-ride scholarship.

BYU also showed interest, and the Cougars had more than a little in their favor. For one thing, they assigned line coach Tom Ramage as Bosco's chief recruiter. Ramage was from Price and had known Lou Bosco at Utah State. For another thing, Robbie had an indelible memory about recent BYU football history. He had been camped in front of the television set in December 1979 when BYU and San Diego State met on national television and watched as Marc Wilson threw four touchdown passes in a 63-14 rout. For yet another thing, John was already going to school at BYU. And if that wasn't enough, Robbie kept remembering the night he'd stood in the middle of the empty stadium.

In the recruiting derby BYU easily took over first place. But there was a hitch. Sean Salisbury, an all-everything quarterback from Escondido, California, was also being recruited by the Cougars. It was obvious they wanted him more than all the other quarterbacks. Head coach LaVell Edwards was recruiting Salisbury personally. Salisbury said he'd either go to BYU or Southern Cal. If Salisbury chose BYU, Bosco could see the handwriting on the wall, and it spelled *understudy* in capital letters. He knew Jim McMahon would be back the next fall, in 1981, for his senior season. He knew there was already a line of quarterbacks behind McMahon, including Gym Kimball and Eric Krzmarzick. And he knew Salisbury wouldn't come to Provo without guarantees.

If Salisbury chose BYU, Robbie decided he would stay in California and go to either Cal-Berkeley or San Diego State.

When letter-of-intent-signing day came along in February, Bosco was still waiting on Salisbury, and so was BYU. Finally, with Edwards and the USC coach in front of him at his home in Escondido, Salisbury made up his mind. He was going to Southern Cal. Ramage, who was staying at the Heritage Motel in Roseville, just down the street from Evelyn Avenue, called Lou and Elva as soon as he got the news.

"Robbie's going to BYU," he said.

1981-1984

If your quality of life is measured by how much sleep you get, the last week of August in the summer of 1984 was easily the worst of Robbie Bosco's twenty-one years.

Each night was the same. He'd stare at the ceiling in his basement apartment on University Avenue in Provo — "The Dungeon," it was called, both affectionately and appropriately — and toss and turn. And then, just after he'd finally dozed off, it was time to get up.

But on Thursday night, August 30, it got ridiculous. He didn't sleep at all. Going to bed had been futile. He called his girlfriend, Karen Holt, and asked her to come over. She did, and she listened for a long time. She was good at listening, and at the moment Robbie Bosco had a lot on his mind — all of it having to do with the football season, which was scheduled to begin in slightly more than twenty-four hours.

Friday morning the BYU team would assemble in front of the Smith Fieldhouse to catch buses to the Salt Lake City International Airport, where they would board a plane bound for Pittsburgh, Pennsylvania. The Cougars were opening the season on the road, at Pitt Stadium, against a University of Pittsburgh team that preseason magazines called "The Beast of the East." The Pitt Panthers were ranked number three in the preseason wire service polls. ESPN had jumped on the chance to showcase The Beast early, and was going to televise the opener.

Not only was BYU opening on national television, and against a top-five team, but it would be Robbie Bosco's first-ever start as a major college quarterback.

He was not handling it well.

No one, and this included Bosco, was questioning the fact that he had paid his dues and won the right to be the BYU starter. The previous spring, after Steve Young had heaped his own impossible career totals on the quarterback mountain, elevating it to newer and unprecedented heights, Bosco engaged in a spirited battle for the top job with Blaine Fowler, a fellow junior-to-be. Fowler, the upstate New York Player of the Year as a high school

179

All-American in Elmira, New York, had backed up Young in 1983, when Young was a junior, and had then redshirted the 1983 season. Bosco had redshirted the 1982 season, and as a third-year sophomore had backed up Young in 1983. In the spring of 1983 Fowler and Bosco alternated at number one and were virtually even as statistics go. Quarterback coach Mike Holmgren and head coach LaVell Edwards ultimately decided on Bosco. It was a hunch more than anything else. They liked the way he threw the ball. His range was remarkable. They thought he had the potential to be the best pure thrower BYU had ever had. At eighteen to twenty yards he was at his best. Plus he was an easy-going, low-key player who was well liked by his teammates.

He wasn't much on the run. In that regard he was the direct opposite of Young. But at 6'3" he had a height advantage (Fowler was 6'0"), and Holmgren went to work adapting the playbook to Bosco's relative immobility. More drop-back plays were added, replacing the sprint-outs that had come into vogue with Young. If Bosco was going to beat anyone, it would be through the air.

In his brief work in 1983, Bosco had looked promising— although you could never trust what happened during mop-up, fourth-quarter blowouts. For the season he completed seventeen of twenty-eight passes for three touchdowns and had thrown just one interception. As a freshman in 1981 he had been named the Most Valuable Offensive player on the freshman team.

Those were his credentials.

Missing from his resume was something all his predecessors at the BYU quarterback position had enjoyed: a sneak preview.

Any quarterback who had inherited the position during the Edwards era had been granted the benefit of a dress rehearsal, as it were. Gifford Nielsen came in as a substitute midway through his sophomore season, and then won the job. Marc Wilson had replaced Nielsen halfway through his sophomore season. Jim McMahon had split time with Wilson before getting the full-time starting job. Steve Young had two starts his sophomore season while McMahon was injured.

Bosco was to be the first in the line to have his first BYU start coincide with the first game of the season. In 1983 Young had been as durable as the Great Wall of China. Only in the eighth game of the season, against Utah State, had Bosco experienced anything close to a test-of-fire. Young had left the game with a concussion with Utah State leading 7-3. Bosco came in for a series, completed three passes in three attempts for twenty-eight yards and a touchdown. Young then came back in and directed a 38-34 win.

Other than that, Bosco's first three years at BYU had been anonymous. He'd settled into college life smoothly enough. He was no library wonder, but he got by in the classroom. When he wasn't studying or watching soap operas, he played sports. As a freshman he teamed with some other football players and his brother John to win the BYU intramural basketball championship.

His sister, Loretta, lived in nearby Payson, and he spent a lot of time there. And he found a steady girlfriend, Karen, with whom he saw every movie that came to Provo.

Robbie lived with his closest friend on the football team, middle linebacker Cary Whittingham, for a while. The Whittingham house had become a kind of football dormitory, housing half-a-dozen players on any given night. Cary's father, Fred, BYU's former defensive coordinator, had moved to Los Angeles to work as an assistant coach with the NFL Rams, and somebody had to sleep in all those bedrooms.

But by his junior year Robbie moved on to live in The Dungeon, alone. Just as the Punt, Pass and Kick contest had suited him, so did living alone. He liked to get dinner at McDonald's, sit back in the couch and eat, and go to sleep.

If things went right, there would be crowds soon enough. After Bosco won the first-string job in the spring of 1984, Steve Young, knowing of his reclusive tendencies, warned Robbie about the members of the media waiting out there. "I'll pass on that end of it," Bosco had said. "Doesn't matter," said Young. "They won't."

Young tried to help by conducting mock interviews with Bosco after practice. He would hold an imaginary microphone while Gordon Hudson or Mike Holmgren posed as cameramen.

"How did it feel out there today?" Young would ask. "Were

you surprised at their blitz?" "How does it feel to take over from the great Steve Young?"

Bosco would let out a low groan that would build, and he'd end the interview with, "Aw, come on."

In the summer of 1984 he returned home to Roseville, where he was left mostly to himself; but by July the media started tracking him down. It was uncovered that Bosco's great-great grandfather had been Wilford Woodruff, the fourth president of the Mormon Church. His mother's maiden name was Woodruff. (Robbie's father was a Catholic, his mother a Mormon, and religious preference was not a factor in his recruiting; he joined the Church at the end of his second semester at BYU.)

Robbie managed to keep the future off his mind most of the time, and had returned to Provo and survived August two-a-days without hyperventilating. If he had anything down cold, it was the BYU offensive system he'd been immersed in for three full years.

But when the final week of fall camp came, and the Cougars were scaling down their workouts to get ready for the Pitt game, reality in all its frankness set in—and he became a candidate for the psyche ward.

He'd lie in bed in The Dungeon thinking, "What if it all ends with Steve Young?"

Other people were also wondering if the succession could go on forever. The media, for instance. Reporters and broadcasters descended on Pittsburgh in droves, intrigued by Pitt's potential and BYU's changing of the guard. The Cougars, despite their eleven-game winning streak and final number-seven ranking at the end of the 1983 season, were ignored by the preseason top twenty polls entirely. Steve Young and Gordon Hudson were gone, along with a number of other senior stars from 1983, including the top three running backs (Casey Tiumalu, Eddie Stinnett and Waymon Hamilton), two of the top three receivers (Mike Eddo and Kirk Pendleton), and defensive standouts Chuck Ehin, Jon Young and Todd Shell.

There was drama here. Bosco had inherited a legacy. Could he keep it alive? One sportswriter, Ian Thomsen, was dispatched to the scene by the *Boston Globe*. This was how Thomsen set the scene in Pittsburgh:

"He was in Pittsburgh, a lonely boy in that crowded hotel room. Always nearby, but only suddenly realized, was the presence of Gary Sheide, the first of the Brigham Young quarterbacks; and of Gifford Nielsen, the first of the All-Americas; and then here came Marc Wilson (the tall one) and Jim McMahon (probably the best one) and Steve Young (the last one).

"And, now, him. The room had been assigned to the next Brigham Young first-string quarterback, and Robbie Bosco was lying in the bed. He really wanted to pack and go home. He really did. This was the night he had worked two seasons and a redshirt year to sleep through, but all he could remember was that 11-year precedent of efficiency and victory and, let's be honest, how long could that continue? The odds said someone had to crash the whole thing sometime — just a nervous jerk of the controls and kaboom — and common sense pointed to it happening against the No. 3 team in the country, here, in Pittsburgh. . . . The cameras here would bounce live pictures off some satellite, and any family equipped with ESPN could say it was there when a BYU quarterback finally messed up."

That was what they were reading in Boston.

When he walked into Pitt Stadium Saturday afternoon, Bosco looked to the heavens for help — and saw the Goodyear Blimp.

The ordeal began.

"Of the first four balls he threw," said Holmgren, "three were maybe the worst balls I've ever seen anybody throw in my whole life."

Bosco was playing like someone who hadn't slept for a week. He wasn't setting his feet to pass. He was throwing the ball too hard and too fast. The Pitt defensive backs were wiping drool off their chins.

The opening series went like this:

First play: Blaine Fowler, playing at halfback, completes a pass to Glen Kozlowski for a short gain.

Second play: Bosco's pass intended for Mark Bellini sails ten yards over his head out-of-bounds.

Third play: Bosco's pass intended for Adam Haysbert almost hits him in the back.

Fourth play: punt.

In the first half the Cougar offense gained eighty-eight yards through the air and scored just three points, on a field goal.

There was one salvation.

The Pitt Panthers didn't score anything.

Maybe they were ranked number three by AP, UPI, and *Sports Illustrated*, and maybe they could boast of the number-one-ranked defense in America over the past five seasons; but as bad as Bosco was in the opening half, the Panther offense was worse.

Pitt's only realistic chance was to win it defensively, which is what appeared would be the case when the second half began and Bosco—after having the intermission to reevaluate who he was and what he was doing—called on his experience from the first half and started up the nightmare all over again. He threw two consecutive interceptions in the third quarter, both of which Pitt turned into touchdowns. The Panthers led 14-3.

It was an odd time to settle down. But now that he really had his work cut out for him, and now that the viewers in ESPN land were thinking about turning the channel, Bosco started looking familiar to the players on the BYU side of the field. He started looking like he looked in practice.

Up to this point Edwards had only spoken to Bosco briefly. "Don't worry," he had told him at halftime. "You're the guy."

BYU got another field goal and then scored a touchdown on the ground. When a try for a two-point conversion failed, Pittsburgh still led, 14-12.

But the Panthers couldn't move the ball and, with 3:05 remaining, BYU got the ball back at its own twenty-six-yard line.

A minute later the ball was resting at midfield and the Cougars faced a third-and-four. Bill Callahan, the Pitt free safety who had victimized Bosco with a seventy-eight-yard touchdown return off an interception earlier in the half, cheated up toward the line of scrimmage, leaving the deep middle zone open. Norm Chow called the play from the press box—a post pattern for the wide receivers, Kozlowski and Haysbert, who would converge from the left and the right. As the secondary receiver on the play, Haysbert's usual job was to clear out the defense and make it easy for Kozlowski underneath. But when the ball was snapped, Callahan cleared himself out by coming underneath. Bosco, by now in full control of his senses, looked first at Callahan and then turned his full attention to Haysbert—whom he knew was now a free man.

Bosco released the pass just as he was hit. On the ground he worried that he hadn't put enough on the ball. But then the crowd went quiet, and he knew without looking that Haysbert had taken the pass in full stride and run into the end zone. BYU had beaten the Beast of the East 20-14.

On the plane ride back to Provo, Bosco stretched out flat on the aisle floor between the seats. He had been hit so hard in the back that he couldn't sit down. The flight attendant cut up his steak in bite-size pieces. This wasn't so bad. He did something he hadn't done in a week: He slept.

A rematch awaited the next weekend with Baylor, the only team to beat BYU the year before. Largely because the entire defense was returning, most preseason rankings put the Bears among the top thirty teams in the country.

It figured that Baylor's defense would try to get to Bosco early, as Pittsburgh had. But what the Baylor defense didn't know, and was about to find out, was that a strong bond had been established in the Pitt game between the new quarterback and an old offensive line.

Four members of the BYU line were returning starters—tackle Louis Wong, guards Robert Anae and Craig Garrick, and center Trevor Matich—and the fifth starter, 270-pound tackle David Wright, was an experienced junior. They had taken great pride in protecting Steve Young the year before, and now were taking even more pride in protecting Bosco, a quarterback who stayed in the pocket and really needed them. It was their tenacity that had given Bosco enough time to spring from his emotional trap in the Pitt game. After the game Bosco bought them a round of candy treats, a tradition that would continue all year. (At the end of the year Bosco bought his offensive line dinner at the Provo

Chuck-A-Rama, a budget all-you-can-eat place that did not make a profit that night.)

Wright, Garrick, Matich, Anae and Wong treated Bosco like the mob treated Capone. They didn't want nobody touching the boss.

The linemen became the team leaders. Buoyed by the win over third-ranked Pitt, they called a players-only team meeting on the Friday night before the Baylor game. The coaches may have been sticking to the "we'll-play-them-one-at-a-time" line, but the players had peeked at the season's full schedule and realized that if they could beat their next two opponents — Baylor and Tulsa, both in Provo — they had a reasonable shot at an undefeated season. The following eight opponents were all WAC schools, a collection of teams that had picked up a combined three wins against the Cougars in the last five years. Then a twelfth regular-season game against Utah State would be the only thing standing in the way of a 12-0 record.

Garrick presided at the team meeting and read a poem he'd read while flushed by the victory over Pitt.

He cleared his throat and began:

> "When things go wrong, as they sometimes will;
> Where the road you trudge seems all uphill;
> When the funds are low and debts are high,
> and you want to smile but you have to sigh;
> When your cares are pressing you down a bit,
> Rest if you must but don't you quit!"

The team responded vociferously — to the sentiment if not the verse.

"We've got a shot at a national championship," said Kozlowski, putting 12 and 0 together. "Hey, they've got to look at us if we go undefeated."

Bosco kept his thoughts to himself. His major college career was one game old, and half of that game had been pure trauma. If his teammates wanted to think about going 12-0 and winning the national championship, fine. But he wasn't waxing poetic just

186

yet. He went into the Baylor game for his home debut in Cougar Stadium as curious as the 63,705 fans in the stands.

Then he threw five touchdown passes—in the first half.

"It was the first time I realized what this offense could do," said Bosco. "That we could score when we wanted to."

Baylor realized the same thing. Bosco threw a touchdown pass to end every drive in the first half—two to Kozlowski, two to Kelly Smith, and one to tight end David Mills. When he added a sixth touchdown pass—to Mills—just four minutes into the fourth quarter, the rout (BYU won 47-13) was official and Bosco, who completed twenty-eight of forty-three passes for 363 yards and didn't throw an interception, did what those who had come before him always did under similar circumstances: He sat down early.

After the game, Baylor coach Grant Teaff met Edwards at midfield. "I hope you're really that good, and we're not that bad," he told him.

The mutual admiration society between Bosco and his offensive line became even more solid. In two games Bosco had come to the realization that he was nothing without those guys. It was a brutal game. Defensive linemen liked to make his life miserable. In the Pitt game the war had been declared. Chris Doleman, a huge Pitt lineman, had knocked Bosco out of the game for one play—he'd had to go to the sidelines to regain his equilibrium. Bosco called his high school buddy in Roseville, Darren Woessner, and told him, "Darren, you've never been hit as hard unless you've been in a car wreck."

The Baylor game provided more introductions to the turf. The line couldn't hold out anybody forever. A strange addition appeared on Bosco's body the morning after—a hump on his lower back the size of a small basketball.

On top of that he got the flu. On Friday morning. The day before game three against Tulsa. It was a fine time to get sick. The BYU Cougars were now ranked number six in the country and had a fourteen-game winning streak, the longest in America. And in addition to the fact that he had an odd growth on his back, Bosco couldn't stand to look at the pregame meal.

Still, he had Friday night to rest. And because Tulsa wasn't rated as the world's best, or even third best, football team, he was able to get some sleep. A bottle of aspirin and several large rolls of tape around his waist got Bosco to the starting line Saturday afternoon. His statistics didn't look sick. He completed twenty-two of thirty-three passes for 314 yards and one touchdown in a 38-15 Cougar Stadium win that showed that this BYU team was more than just a pretty quarterback.

The Cougar defense set up more than half of the offense's points and four times stopped Tulsa inside the BYU twenty-yard line. Bosco had help from everywhere. Then he applied the clinching touchdown late in the third quarter when he pointed to Mills, his tight end, to make a block, and Bosco tucked the ball under his arm and ran thirty-three yards for the first rushing touchdown of his college career.

Now the country's longest winning streak was at fifteen games, and BYU had climbed to number four in the polls. A lot had happened in the three weeks since Bosco looked up in Pittsburgh and gulped when he saw the Goodyear Blimp.

The WAC season was ready to begin, starting with a game at Hawaii—a nice place to visit but you wouldn't want to play a football game there. Bosco had shaken the flu. His new injury of the week was a groin pull, which, when coupled with his bad back, combined for a good deal of pain. But only when he moved. By halftime in Honolulu he looked bad enough that Edwards asked him if he could go on. Bosco mumbled that he could, and he did, but not until just five minutes remained did he get the Cougars past Hawaii with a twenty-five-yard touchdown pass to Kozlowski. The final score was 18-13, and Bosco threw for just 264 yards and one touchdown. Again the defense came to the rescue. A tackle by safety Kyle Morrell on Hawaii quarterback Raphel Cherry midway through the fourth quarter stopped a Hawaii touchdown by inches.

A bye week followed the Hawaii trip, and Bosco had never been happier to *not* play football. He rested his aching back. He rested his pulled groin. At home in The Dungeon he watched "General Hospital," which under the circumstances seemed appropriate. He took his offensive line out for hamburgers.

Two Saturdays later, feeling better than he had since August, he traveled with the Cougars to Colorado State where the R&R continued. Bosco barely played half the game, completing sixteen of twenty-one passes for two touchdowns and running for a third. He participated in a total of just twenty-four plays as the Cougars won easily 52-9.

Not that they would all go so smoothly. Loaded down with The Streak (sixteen games following the CSU win) and their national ranking, the Cougars struggled the next two weeks, having to come from behind to beat Wyoming 41-38 and then sweating out Air Force at Colorado Springs for a 30-25 win during a snowstorm. Bosco took a severe blow to the neck in the Wyoming game — he was starting to feel as though his body had a target on it that moved around weekly — but he threw five touchdown passes nevertheless, including the fourteen-yard game-winner to Mills with just 4:16 remaining. It marked the third come-from-behind, game-winning touchdown pass and drive for Bosco and the Cougars in their first six games. Against an Air Force team that had just returned from South Bend, Indiana, and a win over Notre Dame, Bosco threw for four touchdowns and completed 68 percent of his passes (twenty-eight of forty-one) in spite of a wet field.

The Cougars were 7-0 and counting. If the exact wording of Garrick's poem had been forgotten, Kozlowski's words hadn't: "Hey, they've got to look at us if we go undefeated."

The Cougars next went to New Mexico and won 48-0, and then beat up on UTEP and San Diego State in Provo 42-9 and 34-3 respectively. The winning streak kept mounting and so did the pressure; but in truth, there was nothing hard about these games except the anticipation.

Bosco had thrown seven interceptions all season long, after 362 passing attempts, and two of those had happened during his nervous breakdown in Pittsburgh. In seven games he had already thrown twenty-nine touchdown passes and completed over 62 percent of his passes.

As a result, he went where others had gone before. On the air. He was a guest on "Good Morning America." He was on the nightly news. He was flown to Roseville for a town banquet, with himself as the guest of honor. Scouts were calling him the consummate quarterback. He could throw long, like Sheide. He had a strong arm, like Wilson. He could win, like McMahon. He could read defenses, like Nielsen. He could even run when he had to, like Young.

He did have a tendency to get banged up more than any of the others. For every game he won he had an injury to show for it. He had wraps for every part of his body. He was a training room regular. But he never missed a start, and he never lost—which was more than anyone else in America, in the fall of 1984, could say.

The Cougars were charmed. While they were winning weekly, the rest of the country's top teams were playing college football's version of Russian roulette. Each Sunday the Cougars picked up the newspaper and read the scores to see which contender had taken the week off.

BYU had been unranked when the season began. Teams in the top twenty had included Auburn, Michigan, defending national champion Miami, Pittsburgh, Nebraska, Clemson, UCLA, Texas, Ohio State, Notre Dame, Alabama, Iowa, Penn State, Arizona State, Southern Methodist, Oklahoma, Boston College, Washington, Florida State, and the University of Southern California.

It figured that all these teams had to cooperate by losing sometime during the season. They did. Auburn was the AP preseason number-one pick, but they lost their opening game, against Texas. Then Miami lasted two games at the top before losing to Michigan. Nebraska took over at number one and lasted one week before losing to Syracuse. In the meantime, Purdue was derailing the hopes of undefeated seasons at both Ohio State and Notre Dame; and other early contenders, Pittsburgh and Michigan, lost to BYU and Washington, respectively. Texas, with a 3-0 record, took over the number-one spot from Nebraska, and then tied Oklahoma 15-15.

Washington, streaking along with seven straight wins, became number one, with Oklahoma (5-0-1), Texas (4-0-1), Boston College (4-1), Nebraska (6-1) and SMU (4-1) next in line—ahead of the seventh-ranked (and 7-0) BYU Cougars.

Then Boston College lost to West Virginia by a point, and SMU lost to Houston by a touchdown while BYU was beating Air Force.

Oklahoma lost the next week, allowing BYU to leapfrog to the number-four spot—still behind Washington (now 9-0), Texas (6-0-1) and Nebraska (8-1). Meanwhile, South Carolina, with an 8-0 record, was coming on strong and was ranked number five.

The next weekend Washington and Texas both lost.

Coming into the eleventh game of the season—at Salt Lake City against a good University of Utah team—BYU was ranked number three in the country. Nebraska, at 9-1, was number one, and South Carolina, at 9-0, had jumped ahead of BYU to number two.

Utah had a 6-4-1 record, but on the artificial turf of Rice Stadium the Utes were undefeated through two seasons and ten games. The fact that the Cougars, their arch-rivals, were coming in ranked number three only fueled Utah's incentive, as did rumors that Utah coach Chuck Stobart needed the win to secure his job for another year. Stobart had his team change from the white pants they'd worn during warm-ups into all-red uniforms when they came onto the field for the kickoff. On one of their first plays the Utes tried a double-reverse flea-flicker. They threw everything at the Cougars. And with effectiveness. Going into the fourth quarter BYU had generated enough offense for a bare 17-14 lead.

With time running out, and Utah's defense firing up, the Cougars found themselves facing a third-and-eight midway through the fourth quarter—deep in Utah territory.

No matter what was going on in Lincoln, Nebraska, where the number-one-ranked Cornhuskers were favored to beat Oklahoma. No matter what was going on in Columbia, South Carolina, where the number-two-ranked Fighting Gamecocks were easily favored to beat Navy. The number-three-ranked Cougars had trouble of their own in Salt Lake City.

Bosco called a slant to Kozlowski, who bobbled the ball, grabbed it again, and went fourteen yards for a first down.

Minutes later, there was another long third-down situation—this time third-and-ten. Bosco called for a curl pattern to Kozlowski, who caught the pass and went twenty-nine yards to the four-yard line. Seconds later Kelly Smith caught a touchdown pass—Bosco's third of the day—and BYU sneaked into the locker room with a 24-14 win.

On the bus ride back to Provo they tallied the day's other returns. Navy had upset South Carolina 38-21, and Oklahoma had beaten Nebraska 17-7.

At 11-0, BYU had the only undefeated record in major college football. The poll voters had no choice. When the top twenty came out on Tuesday, November 17, BYU was number one.

With its undefeated record, there had been reason to vote BYU into the top spot earlier in the season. But even if the Cougars had been one of the four winningest programs (along with Oklahoma, Nebraska and Penn State) in America the past ten years, and even if they had turned out All-American quarterbacks like Japan turned out Toyotas, every time they ran a play it was almost as though Woody Hayes and Darrell Royal and Bear Bryant and every other coach who was raised on the run began to politely cough.

Real football teams didn't pass.

Barry Switzer, the coach of the Oklahoma Sooners and not coincidentally the number-two team in the nation, added to the controversy by rapping BYU's schedule. He said BYU hadn't played anybody good and didn't deserve to be number one. Bryant Gumbel, the host of NBC's "Today" show (and a former sportscaster) agreed. He woke up America on Monday morning by saying that BYU played "Bo Diddley Tech," referring to the Cougars' patsy schedule and not to Mr. Bo Diddley, a rhythm-and-blues singer who, when asked about Gumbel's comment, said, "Who's Bryant Gumbel?"

Not that the Cougars didn't have their supporters. ABC sportscaster Keith Jackson joined the public debate and went on record in favor of BYU. The Cougars had played Pittsburgh, after all, when the Panthers had been ranked number three, in Pittsburgh. They had played a good Baylor team that had been given preseason top-thirty consideration. They had beaten the University of Hawaii, the Air Force Academy, and the University of Utah in the WAC, all of whom had winning seasons.

ABC went so far as to conduct a national call-in poll before the next weekend's games. "Should BYU be number one?" The Cougars were supported by 40 percent of the callers, which meant 60 percent of the country had their doubts.

All the Cougars had going for them was a perfect record. In the final game of the regular season, against a 1-9 Utah State team in Provo, they won 38-13 and kept it that way. It was far from Bosco's best day. He threw one touchdown pass and completed twenty-eight of fifty-two passes with one interception. But it was good enough for a 12-0 season. Throughout the game the scoreboard flashed "We're No. 1" in no less than thirty foreign languages, including Oklahoman.

The steady diet of winning had carried a price. The pressure of being on top, for some reason, was more intense than the pressure of being down and out. When Northwestern University was stretching its then-NCAA record of thirty-four consecutive losses earlier in the 1980s, the football players were remarkably resilient. They'd lose on Saturday and then sleep like babies. Yet when Roger Maris, for another example, was chasing Babe Ruth's record of sixty home runs in a season, his hair fell out in clumps.

While Gumbel and Switzer and Jackson were debating the issue of "Who's number one?" and eleven thousand fans in Provo were signing their names to a huge "Congratulations Cougars!" billboard outside Cougar Stadium, Bosco was retreating deeper into The Dungeon. After the Utah State win he disguised himself by wrapping up in a towel, then grabbed his clothes and hurried out the back door of the locker room, dodging the press and the autograph seekers entirely.

HOLIDAY BOWL VII

In San Diego, as the Holiday Bowl approached, solitude was impossible.

When they were sure they would have the nation's top-ranked team in their bowl game, Holiday Bowl officials made last-minute maneuverings. They tried to make a deal with other bowls to get a worthy opponent for BYU, an opponent that would either verify the Cougars' greatness or bury them in San Diego's harbor. Some of the bowls, on the other hand, tried to buy BYU from the Holiday Bowl. The Cotton Bowl wanted to match the Cougars against the Southwest Conference champion in Dallas and was willing to pay more than a million dollars for the privilege. But no deals were struck. And because the bowl-game structure is based solely on money, and has little to do with what's right or wrong or fair for college football, BYU was left to play the best team the Holiday Bowl's relatively meager $500,000 payout could buy.

That meant the Michigan Wolverines, a team that had been ranked as high as number four early in the season but had slumped to 6-5 by season's end.

Because of the bowl-game system, which prohibits a national championship tournament, there is no on-the-field process of actually determining America's football national champion. Those teams invited to bowl games play their contests during the holiday season, after which the final polls are released. The team voted number one is the national champion.

BYU had to keep its votes.

The Cougars' hopes rested upon how well they could look on national television against Michigan. The poll voters would either be watching on TV, or they'd be in the Jack Murphy Stadium press box. The usual press contingent for the Holiday Bowl ballooned to five times its usual size. Newspapers from every part of the country sent reporters.

In the days before the game, everyone wanted to talk to Bosco. The feeling wasn't entirely mutual. Despite the good intentions of Steve Young, and despite a season during which he had ample opportunity to get used to it, Bosco's reaction to microphones remained one of barely concealed horror. He could get in front of sixty-five thousand screaming people, and he was okay. But he didn't feel comfortable talking to groups of people about himself. He was not a great interview. A writer in San Diego asked him about his life-style. "My idea of a good time is sitting at home and going to sleep," he said. Another reporter asked him where he liked to eat. "McDonald's," he said.

Before the Michigan game, which was played at night, Bosco went to a shopping mall in San Diego with his father. They didn't talk much. They didn't buy anything. They did dodge the press, and they did kill time. It suddenly seemed that this season that had happened so quickly was taking forever to end.

Then the fireworks went off and the skydivers landed in the stadium and Holiday Bowl VII began; and before he knew what hit him, Bosco ran into Mike Hammerstein, who was not looking for an interview.

During Bosco's impromptu taping session in the training room — in addition to the sprained ankle and the strained knee, his ribs had been bruised — the cause on the field had been carried forward by Fowler, a veteran of just thirty-four passing attempts all season. But only eight months previous it had been barely more than a coin flip that gave Bosco the job ahead of him, and now he was rather enjoying himself, finally getting a chance to play. He completed four of six passes during a twenty-eight-yard drive that finally ended with a punt.

Mike Holmgren had his headset on early in the second quarter when he sent Fowler out for BYU's next offensive series. The game was still scoreless. Fowler completed his first pass, to David Mills, when Holmgren, through the headset, heard a thunderous cheer. He turned to see Bosco approaching. He was trying not to limp.

"I can play," said Bosco.

"The doctor's got to tell me that," said Holmgren.

"He can play," said Pratley.

As Bosco hobbled to midfield, the 61,243 spectators — at the time the largest crowd ever to see a football game in San Diego — gave him a resounding ovation. Bosco looked around at his teammates in the huddle. "I didn't want to finish early," he said. He called the play and the huddle broke and he stayed where he was. The Cougars hadn't used the shotgun formation all season; but now, with their quarterback doing a Chester imitation, they had no choice. Bosco lined up six yards behind the center. In a game of touch he would have called for a practice hike. But because this was the middle of the Holiday Bowl, they had to do it without a rehearsal—which was unfortunate. Bosco was in the middle of audibilizing out of the play he'd called in the huddle when Matich, the center, snapped the ball. It hit Bosco unawares. At least it was an accurate snap. It bounced off his chest into his hands and he was able to get off a pass, although it fell incomplete.

There was a murmur in the stands, where BYU fans were in the vast majority. (Michigan fans, who only knew directions to the Rose Bowl, hadn't exactly flocked to California.) Was this going to work? A gimpy quarterback and a new shotgun offense, with the national championship on the line?

Bosco answered the question on the next nine plays. He completed four straight passes, threw one incomplete, ran—well, limped—up the middle for a thirteen-yard gain, threw another complete pass, handed off to Lakei Heimuli for a twelve-yard run, and wound it all up with a handoff to Kelly Smith for a five-yard touchdown run.

BYU led 7-0.

To have the quarterback of the nation's top-ranked team dragging his left leg around on nationwide TV while trying to win the national title did not escape the imagination of America. Bosco became an instant inspiration. In the weeks and months after the game, he would receive hundreds of letters and postcards, not to mention proposals of marriage, from all parts of the country.

The problem was, he also inspired Michigan. The Wolverines used Bosco's second entrance as a rallying point in the second and third quarters. Bosco might be showing a lot of courage, but it was at their expense. They didn't want to lose to a gimpy quarterback. Much like the pitcher who threw the pitch that Hank Aaron hit for home run number 715, they didn't want to be an answer to a trivia question—as in, Who did BYU beat to win the 1984 national championship? Thus inspired, the Wolverines increased their intensity level and forged to a 17-10 lead going into the final quarter. BYU helped with five turnovers—two interceptions and three fumbles.

With fourteen minutes to play in San Diego, the Cougars

didn't have Michigan, or Oklahoma, or Washington, where they wanted them. Who knew where they were skidding? Out of the top ten entirely? Out of the top twenty?

The offense took over at its own twenty-yard line. Bosco completed seven passes to five different receivers and then delivered a high arching touchdown pass to Kozlowski in the corner of the end zone that Kozlowski literally stole from Michigan defensive back Erik Campbell. That made it 17-17. Michigan stalled on its next possession, but Bosco threw a third interception when BYU got the ball back. Michigan stalled again. The BYU defense was rising to the occasion. Michigan had 205 yards total offense entering the fourth quarter. At the end of the game the total would be 202.

But where was the BYU offense? A tie would be like kissing the national championship good-bye.

With 4:36 on the clock, BYU took possession at its own seventeen-yard line. Again, Bosco was going where others had gone. Marc Wilson had seventy-nine yards to negotiate in the final 2:06 against Indiana in Holiday Bowl II. Jim McMahon had forty-one yards to negotiate in the final seconds against SMU in Holiday Bowl III. Steve Young had ninety-three yards to negotiate in the final 3:57 against Missouri in Holiday Bowl VI. All had been successful. Then, again, all had two good legs, and none had the national championship on the line.

On first down, Bosco was chased out of the pocket and slid forward nine yards. On second down, Heimuli gained eight yards for a first down.

On the third play of the series, Smith circled around the right end for one yard. On the fourth play, Bosco got off a twenty-yard completion to Mark Bellini. Bellini was tackled by his face mask, which added another fifteen-yard gain.

BYU had made it to the Michigan thirty-yard line.

With the national championship thirty yards away, BYU went after it the best way it knew how.

An eight-yard completion to Heimuli.

A five-yard completion to Smith.

A six-yard completion to Haysbert.

On the next play, Bosco threw to Smith, who looked up early at the four-yard line and dropped the ball.

Now it was third-and-four, with 1:33 left to play. Any other program in America would have gone to the ground, trying to play ball control and, at the worst, set up a game-winning field goal.

BYU called the same pass play to Smith.

Playing now with no discernible limp—"I think I was on pure adrenalin at that point," he said later—Bosco dropped back. Matich and Garrick and Wright and Wong and Anae were giving him protection like a police escort. He thought briefly about just staying behind them and running. But Smith—"a slow white boy who runs great routes," as McMahon would have put it—broke for the sideline and saw an opening upfield. He got to the end zone as Bosco released the pass.

As the referee held up his hands to signal the touchdown, and as the pro-BYU crowd broke into song and dance, Bosco stood motionless, frozen in the moment, enjoying the view for all of them. For Gary Sheide, who had taken Dewey Warren's revolutionary offense and carried the Cougars to their first bowl. For Gifford Nielsen, who had come off the bench against New Mexico to prove the pass could endure. For Marc Wilson, whose seven touchdown passes had kept the cause alive when it could have died at the hands of Bubba Baker on the Colorado plains. For Jim McMahon, whose tenaciousness raised the level of expectations, and accomplishments, beyond anyone else's imagination. For Steve Young, who came from eighth-string to direct the most prolific college offense of all time. And for himself, Robbie Bosco, who, in four improbable months had taken BYU football to the head of the class. "B. Y. U. National Champion" said a banner unfurled high above in Jack Murphy Stadium. Bosco limped off the field. Neither he nor the program had anything left to prove.

1985

What can you possibly do for an encore after winning the national championship? That was the question as the 1985 season opened. The answer was simple: nothing.

198

Certainly losing to UTEP didn't qualify.

The game was in El Paso on the last weekend in October, and nobody saw it coming. Well, that may not be entirely true. There was a rumor that the Miners had tapped into the frequency used by the BYU coaches in their two-way radio communication from the press box to the field. Nothing was ever proven conclusively; but if the case had gone to court, you can bet Robbie Bosco would have been there with exhibit A: the game film showing his four interceptions.

It had been a quarterback's nightmare. Bosco completed just fifteen of thirty-four passes for 151 yards as the Cougars lost 23-16. It was the first sub-two-hundred-yard day for a BYU quarterback in five years — dating back to McMahon's loss to New Mexico on opening day in 1980 — and it was the first BYU loss to the University of Texas-El Paso in fifteen years. It was like Germany losing a border war to Liechtenstein. The Miners lost every other game in 1985, finished 1-10, and fired coach Bill Yung, whose only consolation was that at least he went out with BYU's (phone?) number.

The loss accentuated the fact that Bosco wasn't entirely his old self. The four interceptions brought his season total, after eight games, to fourteen — this from the quarterback who, the year previous, had thrown just eleven interceptions the entire season and had gone through a five-game stretch throwing just one.

The problem was his velocity, or lack thereof. When he let a pass go, no one was sure when it would get where it was going. On a trip home to Roseville prior to the UTEP game, Bosco had gone into the backyard to throw with his dad, as they usually did. Lou Bosco always wore golf gloves to protect his hands. But after a couple of throws he took them off and cast them aside. "I don't need these anymore," he said to Robbie. "What happened?"

What happened was a jarring tackle in the fourth game of the 1985 season, in Philadelphia against Temple University, that crushed Bosco's right shoulder. He had gone back to pass and been met by a ferocious Temple pass rush. His right arm, the one he used to spread butter on toast and pass the football, took the brunt of the pileup. His shoulder was bent backward at an awkward angle. He finished the game, a 26-24 win, with four touchdown passes and 321 yards, but he was in pain.

Thereafter the doctors tried to determine what was wrong, and Robbie and the ice machine were never far apart.

The season had started in grand fashion — with a 28-14 win over Boston College and the Eagle's touted defensive end, Mike Ruth, in the Kickoff Classic. The game — played in The Meadowlands Arena in New Jersey — was shown on nationally syndicated television, and Bosco and Ruth had received most of the pregame attention. A 249-pound senior with Popeye arms and plans to enter the ministry after football, presumably as a form of repentance, Ruth was touted as the best lineman in the country and the front-runner for the Outland Trophy. Bosco was touted as the best quarterback in the country and the front-runner for the Heisman Trophy.

Despite a mostly new BYU offensive line, Ruth didn't get much of Bosco that night in The Meadowlands. The Cougars dominated the game from start to finish, and the passing game used its national forum to fine advantage. Bosco had three touchdown passes and completed thirty-five of fifty-three passes for 508 yards. The New York-area press, who had driven through the Lincoln Tunnel from Manhattan to get a look at the passing wonder who had won the 1984 national championship, drove back to their typewriters and made it official. Robbie Bosco was the number-one Heisman Trophy contender in 1985.

Who could have guessed that at the end of the season Ruth would be the runaway Outland Trophy winner and Bosco would be wondering if there was a doctor in the house?

Such is the nature of football, a contact sport. Bosco and the Cougars lost the next week, to UCLA, in a 27-24 game in Provo that went to the wire. Both teams played excellent football. Gone was the Cougars' twenty-five-game winning streak, the eighteenth longest in NCAA history. But BYU rebounded with a win over nationally-ranked Washington the next week, 31-3. That game was a matchup between the teams that finished one-two in the polls to end the 1984 season, and served as the last unofficial verification of the Cougars' claim to number one. After that, the

Bosco-for-Heisman campaign heated up. The BYU Bookstore printed thousands of "Bosco for Heisman" posters, featuring the QB himself in life-size color. It was about time for a BYU Heisman. BYU's quarterbacks had come close enough for long enough. Sheide finished tenth, Nielsen sixth, Wilson and McMahon both third, Young second; and in 1984 Bosco finished third.

But then came the collision at Temple. Bosco was examined by the BYU team doctors, who finally took a guess and diagnosed his problem as bursitis. They recommended aspirin and rest. But the soreness didn't go away. For the remainder of the season Bosco was the invisible man in practice. He hardly took the field. Fowler would run the offense Monday through Friday. Then on Saturday Bosco would appear, like a Hollywood star who had left the dirty work to the stuntmen, and play until his arm dropped.

It was a tough way to make a living. Bosco was as in the dark about the condition of his shoulder as anyone. He didn't like to talk about it. When Doug Robinson of the *Deseret News*, who covered the Cougars on a regular basis, wrote about Bosco's throwing problems and questioned that the damage to his throwing arm might be serious, Bosco's (and BYU's) response was not to talk to Robinson. Instead, Bosco (and BYU) defended their position — that it was bursitis — through Ray Herbat of the *Salt Lake Tribune*, another writer who covered the team regularly and who could be counted on to deliver the party line.

It wasn't until well after the end of the 1985 season that Bosco was finally looked at by a specialist — the celebrated Dr. Frank Jobe in Los Angeles. Jobe examined the shoulder for five minutes and had him on an operating table. The Temple blow had ripped several tendons and ligaments and partially separated his shoulder. He had played the majority of his senior season with an arm that belonged in a hospital ward.

Still, BYU had beaten Temple. And the Cougars went on the next week to beat Colorado State 42-7. The next week they beat San Diego State 28-0 — a defeat that ironically helped pave the way for Doug Scovil's dismissal as the Aztecs' head coach. Bosco had thrown three touchdown passes in the Colorado State win, and two more in the San Diego State contest. He threw another four at New Mexico in a 45-23 win that saw him complete forty-two of sixty-one passes for 585 yards.

But then came UTEP.

The shock of the loss reverberated around the country and cost Bosco any chance he had for the Heisman Trophy. (He would finish third again.)

But even if his arm wasn't at full strength, he still had his competitiveness, and BYU still had its offense. In many ways, the 1985 season, more than any other, showed off the effectiveness of the BYU offensive system. It took more than a shoulder separation to the quarterback to render it inoperable.

The Cougars were not a happy bunch after UTEP. They took it out on their next two opponents, beating Wyoming 59-0 and Utah State 44-0. Bosco threw just forty passes in the two games combined. They were more than enough. He didn't throw an interception and had five touchdown passes.

Still, he was throwing the ball like it was nitroglycerin, and he was following in the line of the most incredible quarterback string in the history of football dynasties.

It was bound to happen.

He got booed.

In Provo.

In the tenth game of the season, BYU hosted Air Force, a school that, for several years, had been trying to take away the "Best in the West" title from the Cougars. The Falcons had been beating Notre Dame every year, and they had beaten BYU in 1982 in the inaugural game of the expanded Cougar Stadium; but they had lost to BYU in 1983 and 1984. Now, in 1985, the Falcons had the best team in their history. They were 10-0 coming into the BYU game and were ranked number four in the country. Major bowls were considering them. A national championship was a possibility, as was an undefeated season. Getting past BYU and Bosco's rag arm was top priority. Generals and colonels and corporals flew to Provo to see the battle. The stadium was filled to capacity.

And Bosco started out by throwing four interceptions.

After the third one, and after BYU fell to a 21-7 halftime

deficit, the boos began. They were unprecedented. They were the first by BYU fans against a Cougar quarterback. Ever. For the first fifty years no one booed the quarterback, whoever it happened to be. After all, what was the point? And from Gary Sheide onward no one was booed because each quarterback continued to come up with some new and awesome feat. Beyond that, there had always been a certain humility in the stands. BYU fans were nothing if not long-suffering.

But for thirteen seasons now they had been in the grasp of prosperity. When Bosco opened the second half with a ten-yard pass intended for tight end Trevor Molini that sailed over his head and skipped out-of-bounds, frustration got the better part of valor.

Some people did not boo. They were busy yelling, "Bring in Fowler."

Bosco had a problem with his shoulder, but not with his ears. He heard the boos. And they bothered him. But what could he do? He had created this problem, after all. He was finding out that it had been easy replacing Sheide-Nielsen-Wilson-McMahon-Young compared to replacing himself.

Given these circumstances, it hardly seemed the time for a passing clinic. He had a dead arm. Air Force had a national championship for incentive. The natives were restless. Fowler was throwing on the sidelines. So Bosco racked up the balls and ran the table. The Falcons hardly knew what hit them. He soft-armed them into submission. He used all the tricks. He dumped off short passes to his backs. He called audibles at the line of scrimmage when he saw where the defense was lining up. He looked for his third receiver, and his fourth receiver. He stayed in the pocket.

Somewhere, Doug Scovil and Dewey Warren had to be smiling.

The completions came in bunches. BYU's listless first-half offense had transformed itself into something unstoppable. BYU scored three touchdowns on the number-four-ranked team in the country. The winner came when Bosco spotted Vai Sikahema alone in the flat and hit him with a touchdown play that went for sixty-nine yards. Sikahema didn't need gloves to catch the pass. He joked later that he thought it was a punt and he was about to call for a fair catch. He took it in and raced for the end zone, untouched. Back at midfield Bosco raised both arms, including his dead one, in the air, and in the stands the cheering was again unanimous.

The Cougars played out the regular season unbeaten, getting by Utah and Hawaii 38-28 and 25-6, respectively. In total, Bosco set ten NCAA records. The Cougars had gone 11-2 for the season and won the WAC for the tenth straight year. They were invited to the Florida Citrus Bowl in Orlando to play Ohio State.

BYU lost in the Citrus Bowl, 10-7, when a fourth-quarter drive failed at the buzzer. Bosco's last pass floated lazily into the end zone and was intercepted. So he was human, after all.

EPILOGUE

They moved on, of course — all to offers they couldn't afford to refuse. This included the coaches. Doug Scovil went to San Diego State as the head coach. Ted Tollner went to USC as the head coach. Mike Holmgren took a job on the staff of the San Francisco 49ers as the quarterback coach.

The quarterbacks themselves went one by one to the pros. Gary Sheide's tryout with the Cincinnati Bengals was short-lived. It was his bad timing to come along ten years before shoulder surgery had advanced sufficiently to correct his problem. (Jim McMahon and Robbie Bosco's shoulder problems were similar to Sheide's, and both were able to have the problems surgically repaired.) The $30,000 signing bonus he got from the Bengals was Sheide's only pay as a professional football player. He coached football for one season as an assistant at St. Mary's College in California. Then he went to work in a marina developing business on the East Coast. Within a year he was the company president.

The stapling job on Gifford Nielsen's knee held, and he went on to play six NFL seasons with the Oilers in Houston, where he took a liking to pointed boots and Willie Nelson music and, at the peak of his popularity, opened his own ribs restaurant called

"Giff's." After football he moved into broadcasting, anchoring the sports for KHOU, the ABC affiliate in Houston.

Marc Wilson was selected in the first round of the 1980 NFL draft by the Raiders, who were still in Oakland at the time. He was on two Super Bowl championship teams in eight seasons as a Raider, the last in Los Angeles in 1987, and, at the height of his popularity, signed a contract that paid him $1 million a season. He continued his feud with sportswriters — after a year in Los Angeles he stopped talking to the press — and his best (and limited) success came when he wasn't involved in quarterback battles and/or conflicts with his coaches, which wasn't often.

Jim McMahon moved on to more outrageousness with the Chicago Bears, who selected him as the number-three player overall in the 1981 draft. He arrived in Chicago in a stretch limo and stepped onto Michigan Avenue with a beer in his hand. He said his best memory of BYU was leaving. Still, one of the first things he did as a Bear was help implement aspects of the BYU passing game into Chicago's offense. In his fourth year with the Bears he led them to a 46-10 win over New England in Super Bowl XX in New Orleans. McMahon settled into the Chicago suburbs, opened his own restaurant called "McMahon's," wrote an autobiography for Warner Books that lasted twenty-one weeks on the *New York Times* best-seller list, and built a home with a golf hole in the front yard and a racquetball court.

Steve Young was barely three months removed from BYU when he was playing football again — in the newly formed United States Football League, which played its games in the spring. In 1984 Young signed a four-year contract with the Los Angeles Express that included a signing bonus of $2.5 million, a no-interest loan of $1.5 million, a $275,000 bonus for reporting to training camp, a $1,190,000 base salary, $183,000 to a scholarship fund at BYU, and $34.5 million worth of graduated annuities through the year 2027. Total value: $40,148,000. Although he had been projected to be the first player taken in the upcoming NFL draft, he took the Express offer for the obvious reason that it was hard to turn down $40 million. When he returned home to Greenwich after his first season with the Express, Grit had him clean out the garage and mow the lawn. Young only got the up-front part of the Express money before the franchise went out of business. But BYU already had its $183,000 grant—a token of their former quarterback's esteem. Young moved on to the NFL, playing first for the Tampa Bay Buccaneers before being traded to the San Francisco 49ers, where he was reunited with his old quarterback coach, Mike Holmgren, and where he finally bought a new car.

Robbie Bosco was taken in the third round of the 1986 NFL draft by the Green Bay Packers, who signed him to a three-year contract worth $550,000. Immediately after joining the Packers he was placed on injured reserve, where he stayed his first two seasons. His shoulder was operated on by Dr. Frank Jobe in Los Angeles in 1987. Just weeks after Jobe operated on Bosco he operated on Jim McMahon for the same shoulder problem. (McMahon's on-the-field shoulder surgery from his sophomore year in high school had caught up with him.) Shortly after surgery Bosco married Karen Holt, who had helped talk him through the sleepless night before the Pitt game. Because of the shoulder, his future as a football player remained questionable, but financially he felt no pain. Prior to his senior season at BYU he spent $7,000 for an insurance policy with Lloyds of London that provided for a $500,000 payment if he suffered a career-ending injury.

In one way or another, all kept their ties to BYU—including McMahon, who, in the Super Bowl, wore a headband that said "Pluto" on it, in tribute to his friend and teammate, Dan Plater, whose professional career was cut short by a brain tumor. Prominently displayed in McMahon's den in his home in Illinois is the original "Bed of Roses" cartoon that ran in 1981 in *The Daily Universe*.

Marc Wilson lives in Seattle but bought a condominium in Park City, Utah, where he retreats to ski when the football season is over. Steve Young also bought a home in Park City. Nielsen, the only Utah native of the group, lives full time in Houston.

In personality and in playing style, they were as different as they were alike. They came from the East Coast and the West Coast and from across the street. For some reason, however, northern California contributed more than its fair share. Bosco (Roseville), McMahon (San Jose), and Sheide (Antioch) grew up within an hour of each other. Each had his own distinctive style. McMahon and Sheide were brash and confident and thrived on pressure. Young and Bosco were spurred on by the fear of failure. Wilson performed best in tranquility. Nielsen couldn't produce until the opening whistle sounded.

Nielsen and Sheide were extroverts, Bosco and Wilson were introverts. Young was somewhere in between, a self-groomed public figure. McMahon never gave it a thought. They fit into student life differently. Of the three who were not members of the Mormon Church when they came to BYU—McMahon, Sheide, and Bosco—two of them, Sheide and Bosco, joined the Church.

Aside from their individuality, there were many similarities:

They all had strong parents. Each quarterback's mentor was his father, though none of the fathers was overbearing about sports. While they were at BYU, all six called home after every game to talk things over with his dad.

With the exception of Gifford Nielsen (who had five sisters), they all had a brother close to their age, and the relationships were close. Greg Sheide, Mike McMahon, and John Bosco were older brothers who exerted a positive sports influence, as did Steve Young's younger brother, Mike.

None chose football as his number-one sport when he was growing up. They tended to play all sports; if there was a common favorite, it was baseball. Sheide, Wilson, and McMahon went to college still considering baseball as their top choice. Baseball was Steve Young's first love, and both Nielsen and Bosco were all-star Little League baseball players long before they played a down of organized football. Both preferred basketball to football.

Four of the six didn't develop as passers in high school, where their teams played the veer or wishbone and emphasized the running game. Only McMahon and Wilson were in offenses that passed as much as they ran, and Wilson broke his jaw and didn't play the majority of his senior season in high school.

Each of the six had a tendency toward perfectionism, but no one was particularly overwhelmed by himself, or thought he was not expendable. (The road to fortune and glory was never easy.

Wilson almost quit, McMahon and Young almost transferred, and the coaches tried to trade Nielsen back to the basketball team.)

And all six grew up in neighborhoods that were overrun with kids, with sports as the top diversion. There was plenty of friendly competition in San Jose, Antioch, Roseville, Seattle, Greenwich, Provo, and Roy.

The prototype Brigham Young quarterback, then, might look something like this: grows up in a neighborhood with lots of kids; comes from a stable family, with a close relationship with his father; also has a close relationship with a brother; has a tendency toward perfectionism; likes all sports, but has no particular affection for football; and doesn't develop as a passer until he goes to college.

That kind of a combination worked for thirteen straight seasons at BYU — when the Cougars turned out six of the best quarterbacks to ever play the game.

All told, over thirteen seasons they threw for 43,663 yards and 367 touchdowns while winning 122 games and losing just thirty-six. They set, and reset, 112 NCAA passing and total offense records as their teams won eight national passing titles and five total offense titles. Through the 1987 college football season, BYU held the distinction of having the most prolific offensive team in college history (the 1983 team, with a per-game average of 584.2 yards) and the most prolific passing team in college history (the 1980 team, with a per-game average of 409.8 yards).

Conservative estimates speculate that more than ten thousand athletes have played quarterback on the major-college level since the first college game in 1867. Of the more than three thousand quarterbacks who have played since the end of World War II in 1945, meticulous statistical records have been kept by the NCAA, which has devised a quarterback rating formula that considers all aspects of the passing game — including attempts, completions, interceptions, passing percentage, yards gained, and touchdowns.

As of 1987, Gary Sheide, Gifford Nielsen, Marc Wilson, Jim McMahon, Steve Young, and Robbie Bosco occupied six of the top seventeen spots on the all-time career passing efficiency list. McMahon's 156.9 rating ranked first, Young's 149.8 ranked third,

Bosco's 148.9 ranked fifth, Nielsen's 145.3 ranked eighth, Sheide's 138.8 ranked fifteenth, and Wilson's 137.2 ranked seventeenth.

On the walls of his office in the Smith Fieldhouse at BYU, there is no chart showing the top seventeen quarterbacks in NCAA history. There is an autographed picture of Willie Nelson, which ranks as LaVell Edwards' most prized spoil from the 1984 national championship season. After that season he spent three months enduring a round of almost continuous banquets and receptions (including one at the White House) where he met the rich and famous.

There is only subtle reference to the eleven WAC championships in thirteen years, including ten straight from 1976-1985. Pictures of those teams are on the walls. Looking at the quarterbacks, Edwards remembered their particular talents:

Gary Sheide: "The image of Joe Namath. He even had Joe's number. Had just a great feel and touch for the game. A great athlete who could play all the sports. He was more of a streak guy than any of them. He could miss two or three passes and then get hot and hit ten straight. He was the one who got it all started."

Gifford Nielsen: "He was never a very good practice player. He couldn't run, he didn't have a great arm, he was kind of gangly, but he was sharp as a whip. Such a competitor. As good as we ever had. He had the intangibles that certain leaders have. A presence, an awareness. They're best under pressure. Like Mel Tillis, he talks and he stutters, but when he sings it's completely different. It was like that with Giff. On the field, something just clicked."

Marc Wilson: "He probably had more grace and form and style than anybody I've seen who's 6'5". He played like he was 6'1". A very fluid athlete. He had great speed. Look at the pictures of him. Everything's symmetric. His back is straight, his knees are bent, his feet are in the right direction. Just a terrific athlete. And highly intelligent. He wasn't a real take-charge guy. He had a kind of high-pitched voice, and that sort of compounded his image problem. But he was much more competitive and tougher than you thought. In his quiet way he'd always get it done."

Jim McMahon: "A great natural leader. Great ability. Great presence. For a guy who was supposed to be blind in one eye, he had as much vision as anyone I've ever seen. He'd know instinctively where he should turn and where he should throw the ball. He was never a problem on the field. He was kind of cocky, but that didn't bother me. He had such a quick delivery and such a natural ability. I told Chicago he'd win them a Super Bowl."

Steve Young: "Here's a guy that is really a talent. He's the best athlete we ever had. He could run, he developed into a good thrower. He's smart. He's intense. He could make it in the movies. Really, he's got it all. He was coachable, but he had his own ideas. He never let up, not even in practice. I'd take Steve Young every year."

Robbie Bosco: "One of my all-time favorite people. He never changed from the day he came here to the day he left. He's a very happy guy, laid-back, casual, kind of self-effacing. Yet look at that Michigan game. That was one of the guttiest performances in the history of anything. All those games during the championship season when we had to come from behind to win. He could reach back and find whatever he needed to win. He could run, he could throw, the other players wanted to come through for him. He did it all."

Through the thirteen seasons, Edwards had often been overshadowed by quarterbacks and quarterback coaches, but he had been the only part of the program that was not interchangeable. He had been the lone constant. He watched each quarterback come in without fanfare—none of them were heavily recruited—and leave four or five years later as All-Americans appearing on the morning news shows. It was the same with the quarterback coaches, who came in needing work and left needing agents.

When he got the head job in 1972, it was as much out of default as anything else. No self-respecting coach who already had a job would think of going to BYU. Edwards had been coaching on the high school level or as a Cougar assistant for almost twenty years and had experienced just six winning seasons. He didn't have a great resume, and he didn't have many answers — except one. He knew that a private school in the remote Rocky Mountains with a chronic case of losing needed something revolutionary to have a chance.

The passing game had just sort of evolved. He brought in the technicians and got out of their way. There were times when it looked like it wouldn't fly. In the early part of the 1974 season, when Colorado State tied the Cougars in the final seconds and the team stood at 0-3-1, Edwards thought the great passing experiment was about to collapse under its own weight. That was the lowest point. Edwards felt like the Wright brothers after their thirty-first consecutive crash.

But then BYU won seven straight games and went to its first bowl game.

In 1974, before Gifford Nielsen came from third string to the rescue against New Mexico, he had also had his doubts; and in 1978, when Wally English divided the team, Edwards lost a momentary grip. That season remains the most ironic of them all. The Cougars had Jim McMahon and Marc Wilson on the same team — two players who would become starters in the NFL — and they went through the season unranked and in turmoil. By all accounts it was the worst year of the thirteen, statistically and otherwise. Edwards determined that he would never again have an in-season question about who the starting BYU quarterback was. The next two years, with Wilson and McMahon each taking his own season, the Cougars won twenty-three games and lost two.

Before you knew it, Michigan was going backward in the 1984 Holiday Bowl, and the polls were paying BYU the ultimate "We're Number One" compliment.

The coach had his own offers to leave. None was quite in a league with Steve Young's $40 million offer, but they weren't minimum wage either. The first offer came in 1976, when BYU was playing in the Tangerine Bowl and Miami waved a five-year, $350,000 deal in front of Edwards. After that, in later years, Illinois tried to hire him away, as did Iowa State and Missouri and Colorado and Arizona and Minnesota and Arizona State. Minnesota offered a package deal that, after figuring in television and radio and speaking fees with the base salary, projected to better than $230,000 a year. Arizona's deal was in excess of $200,000 a year, Arizona State's was in excess of $250,000. When the USFL was formed, Denver and New Jersey wondered if he was interested, and the Los Angeles Express wanted him to come in tandem with Steve Young. Immediately after winning the national championship, the Detroit Lions of the National Football League offered him their head coaching job over the phone, and he could name his terms.

More flattering than the money were the coaches the teams hired as their second choices—Howard Schnellenberger at Miami (who went on to win a national championship), Lou Holtz at Minnesota (who later was hired at Notre Dame), Mike White at Illinois, Dick Tomey at Arizona, Bill McCartney at Colorado, John Cooper at Arizona State (who went on to win the Rose Bowl), Darryl Rodgers at the Detroit Lions.

But did Edison leave the light bulb? Did Ford leave the automobile? Did Eli Whitney leave the cotton gin? How could LaVell Edwards leave his invention? He had been the first coach to win consistently with the forward pass and had changed the face of football in the process. Since 1972 he had won more regular-season games than any college coach in America.

As with the Mings and the New York Yankees, the dynasty hadn't lasted forever. In 1986 and 1987, for the first time in more than a decade, quarterbacks played at BYU who were *not* named All-Americans, and the Cougars *didn't* win the WAC.

But the job hadn't come with guarantees. The coach knew that up front. The defenses were never going to just give up. That was the game, and why they played it. LaVell Edwards turned from the photographs of the quarterbacks behind him and looked out his office window. Players were on their way to the practice field. He got up and joined them.

Appendix

GARY SHEIDE

1973	RUSHING					PASSING						TOT.
OPPONENT	CAR.	GN.	LS.	NET.	TD.	ATT.	COM.	%	INT.	YDS.	TD.	OFF.
Colorado State	DID	NOT	PLAY									
Oregon State	0	0	0	0	0	1	1	1000	0	68	1	68
Utah State	0	0	0	0	0	10	6	.600	0	57	0	57
Iowa State	11	25	67	-42	0	41	29	.707	4	439	3	397
Arizona State	4	0	25	-25	0	39	22	.564	1	170	1	145
Wyoming	7	38	10	28	1	38	17	.447	1	310	2	338
New Mexico	3	12	0	12	1	50	32	.640	1	408	6	420
Arizona	10	27	15	12	1	19	10	.526	2	82	0	94
Weber State	1	0	8	-8	0	33	20	.606	2	244	4	236
Utah	2	0	4	-4	0	35	23	.657	0	354	4	350
Texas-El Paso	7	30	10	20	2	28	17	.607	1	218	1	238
TOTALS	42	132	135	-3	5	294	177	.602	12	2,350	22	2,343
1974												
Hawaii	9	11	18	-7	0	22	13	.590	4	154	1	147
Utah State	9	17	34	-17	0	28	18	.642	4	170	0	153
Iowa State	7	10	42	-32	0	11	4	.363	0	23	0	-7
Colorado State	10	9	42	-33	0	14	11	.785	0	123	3	90
Wyoming	4	1	23	-22	0	28	20	.714	0	263	2	241
Texas-El Paso	3	0	8	-8	0	40	27	.675	1	388	5	380
Arizona	2	0	19	-19	0	35	20	.571	0	267	5	248
Air Force	3	0	20	-20	0	30	18	.600	2	213	2	193
Arizona State	2	0	5	-5	0	41	24	.585	5	223	2	218
New Mexico	6	11	12	-1	2	29	15	.517	2	244	1	243
Utah	2	1	2	-1	1	22	11	.500	1	104	2	104
TOTALS	57	60	225	-165	3	300	181	.603	19	2,174	23	2,010

GIFFORD NIELSEN

1975	RUSHING					PASSING						TOT.
OPPONENT	CAR.	GN.	LS.	NET.	TD.	ATT.	COM.	%	INT.	YDS.	TD.	OFF.
Bowling Green	DID	NOT	PLAY									
Colorado State	DID	NOT	PLAY									
Arizona State	2	0	17	-17	0	11	4	.363	1	38	0	21
New Mexico	4	6	0	6	0	12	10	.833	0	148	2	154
Air Force	12	23	32	-9	0	19	14	.737	1	229	1	220
Wyoming	11	22	21	1	0	19	9	.474	1	159	1	160
Arizona	6	11	31	-20	1	44	27	.614	2	387	2	367
Utah State	7	9	42	-33	0	24	15	.625	0	139	2	106
Utah	6	11	23	-12	1	15	10	.666	1	150	1	138
Texas-El Paso	5	1	47	-46	0	24	13	.542	0	157	0	111
So. Mississippi	4	7	21	-14	0	12	8	.666	1	64	1	50
TOTALS	57	90	234	144	2	180	110	.611	7	1471	10	1327
1976												
Kansas State	7	9	24	-15	0	29	15	.517	2	142	0	127
Colorado State	7	0	56	-56	0	33	13	.394	1	172	4	116
Arizona	9	11	23	-12	0	28	18	.643	1	200	2	188
San Diego State	6	9	21	-12	0	25	10	.400	2	80	0	68
Wyoming	9	15	49	-34	0	42	24	.571	2	324	3	290
So. Mississippi	4	5	11	-6	0	31	23	.742	2	445	3	439
Utah State	4	6	19	-13	0	48	28	.583	2	468	5	455
Arizona State	5	11	26	-15	0	37	20	.541	2	339	2	324
Texas-El Paso	7	10	46	-36	0	29	15	.517	1	319	4	283
New Mexico	13	21	71	-50	0	35	17	.486	1	288	3	238
Utah	6	6	30	-24	1	35	24	.686	3	415	3	391
TOTALS	77	103	376	-273	1	372	207	.556	19	3192	29	2919
1977												
Kansas State	7	7	28	-21	0	45	27	.600	0	318	2	297
Utah State	5	22	6	16	0	40	30	.750	0	321	6	337
New Mexico	8	37	38	-1	0	23	19	.826	0	273	5	272
Oregon State	9	22	41	-19	0	48	22	.458	3	255	3	236
INJURED REST OF SEASON												
TOTALS	29	88	113	-25	0	156	98	.628	3	1167	16	1142

216

MARC WILSON

1977	RUSHING					PASSING						TOT.
OPPONENT	CAR.	GN.	LS.	NET.	TD.	ATT.	COM.	%	INT.	YDS.	TD.	OFF.
Kansas State	2	8	0	8	0	9	8	.889	0	101	1	109
Utah State	3	13	15	-2	0	7	7	1000	0	52	1	50
New Mexico	4	5	23	-18	0	4	3	.750	0	29	0	11
Oregon State	1	6	0	6	0	0	0	0	0	0	0	6
Colorado State	8	26	21	5	1	25	15	.600	1	332	7	337
Wyoming	10	20	9	11	0	26	10	.385	6	96	1	107
Arizona	11	11	23	-12	0	43	23	.535	2	334	2	322
Utah	8	31	20	11	0	41	26	.634	3	571	5	582
Arizona State	15	51	45	6	0	38	21	.553	3	283	1	289
Long Beach	12	32	31	1	0	54	37	.685	1	408	4	409
Texas-El Paso	7	29	25	4	1	30	14	.467	2	212	2	216
TOTALS	81	232	212	20	2	277	164	.592	18	2418	24	2438
1978												
Oregon State	12	10	51	-41	0	38	15	.394	3	193	1	152
Arizona State	10	9	55	-46	0	42	17	.405	4	261	0	215
Colorado State	7	32	15	17	0	10	6	.600	1	45	0	62
New Mexico	18	75	31	44	0	39	24	.615	1	293	1	337
Utah State	8	29	17	12	0	18	7	.388	1	57	0	69
Oregon	9	13	24	-11	0	21	10	.476	2	81	0	70
Texas-El Paso	3	13	11	2	0	2	2	1000	0	38	0	40
Wyoming	3	16	0	16	1	3	3	1000	0	44	1	60
San Diego State	3	2	15	-13	0	3	2	.667	0	9	0	-4
Utah	0	0	0	0	0	0	0	0	0	0	0	0
Hawaii	17	92	31	61	1	30	21	.700	0	291	2	352
Nev-Las Vegas	14	73	29	44	0	27	14	.518	1	187	3	231
TOTALS	104	364	279	85	2	233	121	.519	13	1499	8	1584
1979												
Texas A&M	6	6	32	-26	0	35	17	.486	3	165	2	139
Weber State	3	0	19	-19	0	43	21	.488	2	361	1	342
Texas-El Paso	10	8	54	-46	0	44	26	.591	2	340	2	294
Hawaii	4	7	20	-13	1	49	28	.571	1	342	3	329
Utah State	6	25	19	6	0	25	19	.760	0	372	2	378
Wyoming	4	17	8	9	0	48	33	.688	0	448	4	457
New Mexico	5	24	8	16	0	45	21	.467	1	366	4	382
Colorado State	4	5	9	-4	0	40	24	.600	1	358	3	354
Long Beach	10	24	53	-29	0	39	24	.615	1	316	3	287
Utah	5	6	23	-17	0	37	23	.622	1	374	1	357
San Diego State	4	6	23	-17	1	21	13	.619	3	278	4	261
TOTALS	61	128	268	-140	3	427	250	.585	15	3720	29	3580

JIM MCMAHON

1977	RUSHING					PASSING						TOT.
OPPONENT	CAR.	GN.	LS.	NET.	TD.	ATT.	COM.	%	INT.	YDS.	TD.	OFF.
Kansas State	PUNT	ONLY										
Utah State	1	0	0	0	0	1	1	1000	0	6	0	6
New Mexico	PUNT	ONLY										
Oregon State	PUNT	ONLY										
Colorado State	3	3	23	-20	0	3	2	.667	1	14	0	-6
Wyoming	PUNT	ONLY										
Arizona	0	0	0	0	0	3	1	.333	0	6	0	6
Utah	0	0	0	0	0	2	2	1000	0	12	0	12
Arizona State	PUNT	ONLY										
Long Beach	2	0	15	-15	0	0	0	0	0	0	0	-15
Texas-El Paso	1	15	0	15	0	7	4	.571	0	65	1	80
TOTALS	7	18	38	-20	0	16	10	.625	1	103	1	83
1978												
Oregon State	PUNT	ONLY										
Arizona State	PUNT	ONLY										
Colorado State	12	90	10	80	1	9	7	.778	1	112	1	192
New Mexico	PUNT	ONLY										
Utah State	13	83	12	71	0	11	5	.454	1	62	0	133
Oregon	6	18	8	10	0	19	10	.526	0	204	1	214
Texas-El Paso	20	85	23	62	0	19	10	.526	1	143	1	205
Wyoming	13	54	5	49	2	36	24	.667	1	317	1	366
San Diego State	17	31	54	-23	1	29	11	.379	3	174	1	151
Utah	12	76	64	12	0	38	15	.395	0	249	1	261
Hawaii	DID	NOT	PLAY									
Nev-Las Vegas	6	7	20	-13	0	15	5	.333	1	46	0	33
TOTALS	99	444	196	248	4	176	87	.494	8	1307	6	1555
1980												
New Mexico	11	11	55	-44	0	25	11	.440	1	147	2	103
San Diego	4	2	9	-7	0	30	19	.633	1	373	4	366
Wisconsin	5	12	9	3	1	34	22	.647	0	337	3	340
Long Beach	13	32	46	-14	0	42	25	.595	1	339	4	325
Wyoming	4	15	0	15	0	31	22	.710	2	408	4	423
Utah State	10	40	9	35	2	33	21	.636	3	485	6	516
Hawaii	8	23	20	3	0	60	31	.517	3	389	2	392
Texas-El Paso	2	12	10	2	0	36	28	.778	1	451	6	453
No. Texas State	8	24	28	-4	0	50	40	.800	3	464	3	460
Colorado State	10	35	34	1	0	33	23	.697	1	441	5	442
Utah	8	53	26	27	1	34	21	.618	1	399	3	426
Nev-Las Vegas	12	84	41	43	2	37	21	.568	1	338	5	381
TOTALS	95	343	287	56	6	445	284	.638	17	4,571	47	4,627

STEVE YOUNG

1981	RUSHING					PASSING						TOT.
OPPONENT	CAR.	GN.	LS.	NET.	TD.	ATT.	COM.	%	INT.	YDS.	TD.	OFF.
Cal-Long Beach	3	19	4	15	0	8	5	.625	0	47	0	62
Air Force	2	10	0	10	0	1	1	1000	0	14	0	24
Texas-El Paso	3	0	22	-22	0	8	3	.375	0	31	1	9
Colorado	4	75	14	61	0	10	4	.400	0	63	2	124
Utah State	21	102	39	63	0	40	21	.525	1	307	1	370
Nev-Las Vegas	12	89	23	66	0	40	21	.525	4	269	1	335
San Diego State	0	0	0	0	0	1	0	.000	0	0	0	0
Wyoming	DID	NOT	PLAY ————————									
New Mexico	3	13	2	11	0	2	1	.500	0	0	0	11
Colorado State	1	7	0	7	0	0	0	.000	0	0	0	7
Hawaii	DID	NOT	PLAY ————————									
Utah	4	22	0	22	0	2	0	.000	0	0	0	22
TOTALS	53	337	104	233	0	112	56	.500	5	731	5	964
1982												
Nev-Las Vegas	13	40	19	21	1	26	19	.730	1	271	1	292
Georgia	7	17	32	-15	0	46	22	.478	6	285	1	270
Air Force	12	97	0	97	3	28	19	.679	0	215	1	312
Texas-El Paso	13	126	29	97	0	32	24	.750	2	399	2	496
New Mexico	17	33	43	-10	1	28	18	.643	0	336	2	326
Hawaii	4	15	0	15	0	32	22	.688	3	302	2	317
Colorado State	9	107	17	90	2	36	19	.528	4	259	2	349
Utah State	7	26	35	-9	0	38	17	.447	1	223	2	214
Wyoming	13	52	35	17	1	32	24	.750	0	272	1	289
San Diego State	13	112	18	94	2	35	22	.629	1	284	2	378
Utah	6	15	5	10	0	34	24	.750	0	254	2	264
TOTALS	114	640	233	407	10	367	230	.627	18	3100	18	3507
1983												
Baylor	13	143	30	113	2	38	23	.610	0	351	1	464
Bowling Green	9	53	27	26	2	40	30	.750	1	384	5	410
Air Force	7	24	29	-5	0	49	39	.796	0	486	3	481
UCLA	14	67	13	54	0	36	25	.694	3	270	2	324
Wyoming	4	32	0	32	0	39	23	.590	1	356	2	388
New Mexico	5	31	0	31	0	30	24	.800	1	340	4	371
San Diego State	9	67	16	51	2	45	32	.711	0	446	3	497
Utah State	19	104	38	66	1	39	25	.641	1	331	2	397
Texas-El Paso	10	60	10	50	1	43	30	.698	1	359	3	409
Colorado State	7	32	0	32	0	45	33	.733	2	311	2	343
Utah	5	10	16	-6	0	25	22	.880	0	268	6	262
TOTALS	102	623	179	444	8	429	306	.713	10	3902	33	4346

ROBBIE BOSCO

1983	RUSHING					PASSING						TOT.
OPPONENT	CAR.	GN.	LS.	NET.	TD.	ATT.	COM.	%	INT.	YDS.	TD.	OFF.
Baylor	DID	NOT	PLAY									
Bowling Green	1	1	0	1	0	7	3	.428	0	16	1	17
Air Force	DID	NOT	PLAY									
UCLA	DID	NOT	PLAY									
Wyoming	DID	NOT	PLAY									
New Mexico	1	0	7	-7	0	6	6	1000	0	128	1	121
San Diego State	3	7	7	0	0	1	0	.000	0	0	0	0
Utah State	0	0	0	0	0	3	3	1000	0	28	1	28
UTEP	1	0	7	-7	0	7	2	.285	1	43	0	36
Colorado State	DID	NOT	PLAY									
Utah	4	2	15	-13	0	4	3	.750	0	37	0	24
TOTALS	10	10	36	-26	0	28	17	.607	1	252	3	226
1984												
Pittsburgh	11	38	19	19	0	43	25	.581	2	325	1	344
Baylor	6	21	34	-13	0	43	28	.651	0	363	6	350
Tulsa	7	42	21	21	1	33	22	.667	0	314	1	335
Hawaii	8	5	38	-33	0	33	18	.545	1	264	1	231
Colorado State	3	7	4	3	1	21	16	.762	0	246	2	249
Wyoming	8	23	8	15	0	44	29	.659	0	384	5	399
Air Force	8	16	23	-7	0	41	28	.683	1	484	4	477
New Mexico	7	35	26	9	0	29	19	.645	0	227	3	236
UTEP	1	0	0	0	0	31	19	.613	1	237	4	237
San Diego State	8	15	32	-17	0	44	24	.545	2	326	2	309
Utah	7	35	5	30	0	44	27	.614	3	367	3	397
Utah State	11	54	24	30	0	52	28	.538	1	338	1	368
TOTALS	85	291	234	57	2	458	283	.618	11	3875	33	3932
1985												
Boston College	5	4	42	-38	0	53	35	.660	4	508	3	470
UCLA	10	25	37	-16	1	41	29	.707	2	340	2	324
Washington	3	3	17	-14	0	37	23	.622	2	279	0	265
Temple	5	1	16	-15	0	36	24	.667	1	321	4	306
Colorado State	0	0	0	0	0	49	38	.776	0	417	3	417
San Diego State	1	1	0	1	1	37	25	.676	2	257	2	258
New Mexico	7	7	52	-45	0	61	42	.689	3	585	4	540
UTEP	6	16	1	15	0	34	15	.441	4	151	1	166
Wyoming	6	36	12	24	0	21	17	.809	0	266	3	290
Utah State	4	28	9	19	0	19	14	.737	0	220	2	239
Air Force	10	12	80	-68	0	49	29	.592	4	343	3	275
Utah	6	48	15	33	0	37	22	.595	1	276	1	309
Hawaii	4	0	28	-28	0	37	25	.676	1	310	2	282
TOTALS	67	177	309	-132	2	511	338	.661	24	4273	30	4141

YEAR BY YEAR

PLAYER	YEAR	GAMES	ATT.	COMP.	INT.	PCT.	YDS.	TD	CPG	PASS EFF.	NCAA RANKING
Gary Sheide	1973	10	294	177	12	.602	2,350	22	17.7	143.8	2nd
Gary Sheide	1974	11	300	181	19	.603	2,174	23	16.5	133.8	2nd
Gifford Nielsen	1975	9	180	110	7	.611	1,471	10	12.2	140.3	10th
Gifford Nielsen	1976	11	372	207	19	.556	3,192	29	18.8	143.2	4th
Gifford Nielsen	1977	4	156	98	3	.628	1,167	16	24.5	155.1	Injured
Marc Wilson	1977	11	277	164	18	.592	2,418	24	14.9	148.1	8th
Marc Wilson	1978	10	233	121	13	.519	1,499	8	11.0	106.1	—
Jim McMahon	1978	10	176	87	8	.494	1,307	6	7.9	113.9	—
Marc Wilson	1979	11	427	250	15	.585	3,720*	29	22.7	147.1	4th
Jim McMahon	1980	12	445	284	18	.638	4,571*	47*	23.7	176.9*	1st
Jim McMahon	1981	10	423	272	7	.643	3,555	30	27.2	155.0	1st
Steve Young	1981	9	111	56	5	.504	731	5	6.2	111.6	—
Steve Young	1982	11	367	230	18	.627	3,100	18	20.9	140.0	6th
Steve Young	1983	11	429	306	10	.713*	3,902	33	27.8	168.4	1st
Robbie Bosco	1984	12	458	283	11	.618	3,875	33	23.6	151.8	2nd
Robbie Bosco	1985	13	511*	338*	24	.661	4,273	30	26.0	146.4	7th

*NCAA records at the time

All-time NCAA Passing Efficiency

(Through 1987 season)   (Minimum 325 completions)

PLAYER	TEAM	YEARS	ATT.	CMP.	INT.	PCT.	YDS.	TD	PTS.
1. Jim McMahon	BYU	1977-78, 80-81	1060	653	34	.616	9536	84	156.9
2. Vinny Testaverde	Miami (Fla.)	1982, 84-86	674	413	25	.613	6058	48	152.9
3. Steve Young	BYU	1981-83	908	592	33	.652	7733	56	149.8
4. Jim Harbaugh	Michigan	1983-86	582	368	19	.632	5215	31	149.6
5. Robbie Bosco	BYU	1983-85	997	638	36	.640	8400	66	149.4
6. Danny White	Arizona St.	1971-73	649	345	36	.532	5932	59	148.9
7. Chuck Long	Iowa	1981-85	1072	692	46	.646	9210	64	147.8
8. Gifford Nielsen	BYU	1975-77	708	415	29	.586	5833	55	145.3
9. Tom Ramsey	UCLA	1979-82	691	411	33	.595	5844	48	143.9
10. Jerry Rhome	Tulsa, SMU	1961, 63-64	713	448	23	.628	5472	47	142.6
11. Doug Gaynor	Long Beach	1984-85	837	569	35	.680	6793	35	141.6
12. Jim Karsatos	Ohio State	1983-86	573	330	19	.576	4698	36	140.6
13. Jerry Tagge	Nebraska	1969-71	581	348	19	.599	4704	33	140.1
14. John Elway	Stanford	1979-82	1246	774	39	.621	9349	77	139.3
15. Gary Sheide	BYU	1973-74	594	358	31	.603	4524	45	138.8
16. Don McPherson	Syracuse	1983-86							138.1
17. Marc Wilson	BYU	1977-79	937	535	46	.571	7637	61	137.2
18. Randall Cunningham	UNLV	1982-84	1029	597	29	.580	8020	59	136.8
19. Sam King	UNLV	1979-81	625	360	29	.576	5393	30	136.6
20. Dave Yarema	Michigan St.	1982-86	727	447	29	.615	5569	41	136.5

Index